WORLD LITERATURE

INTERACTIVE

Teacher Guide

Novel Companion

Things Fall Apart
Chinua Achebe

Death Comes for the Archbishop
Willa Cather

Nectar in a Sieve
Kamala Markandaya

Cyrano de Bergerac
Edmond Rostand

Picture Bride
Yoshiko Uchida

All Quiet on the Western Front
Erich Maria Remarque

Photo Credits

10 Margaret Courtney-Clarke/CORBIS; **20** Bettmann/CORBIS; **32** Bradley Smith/CORBIS; **42 52** Hulton-Deutsch Collection/CORBIS; **62** Ansel Adams Publishing Rights Trust/CORBIS.

Acknowledgments

Grateful acknowledgment is given to authors, publishers, photographers, museums, and agents for permission to reprint the following copyrighted material. Every effort has been made to determine copyright owners. In case of any omissions, the Publisher will be pleased to make suitable acknowledgments in future editions.

Send all inquiries to:
Glencoe/McGraw-Hill
8787 Orion Place
Columbus, OH 43240-4027

ISBN: 978-0-07-889165-6
MHID: 0-07-889165-5

Printed in the United States of America.

1 2 3 4 5 6 7 8 9 047 14 13 12 11 10 09 08

TABLE OF CONTENTS

Unit 1

Unit 2

Unit 3

The *Novel Companion* is the advanced level of Glencoe's interactive reading workbooks, *Interactive Read and Write*, which accompany the literature program, *Glencoe Literature*. Students will study six novels, autobiographies, and plays as they complete the *Novel Companion* workbook. Each title they study is paired with one unit of *Glencoe Literature*. The titles, chosen from those offered in Glencoe's *Literature Library*, represent well-known and much-loved literature both from the literary canon and from award-winning modern works. They challenge advanced students by offering readabilities that are either at grade level or one grade above level.

The *Novel Companion* workbook does not include the full text of the novels (and the other longer works). Each student should have easy access to their own copies of the novels. The *Novel Companion* does include numerous excerpts from the novels. These excerpts allow students to do close readings of the text as they study key aspects of the novel that reflect important concepts already covered in *Glencoe Literature*.

Connection to the *Glencoe Literature* Program

The major themes and concepts represented by the literary works featured in the *Novel Companion* have been carefully matched to *Glencoe Literature's* Big Ideas, the major themes and concepts that appear in each unit of the *Glencoe Literature* program. The *Novel Companion's* approach to teaching literature and reading is also modeled after that of *Glencoe Literature*: students study

literary elements, apply reading strategies, learn new vocabulary, write about literature, and engage in other activities related to the literature. The *Novel Companion*, however, additionally teaches students note-taking techniques to help them make connections between the *Novel Companion's* longer works and *Glencoe Literature's* shorter works.

Although the *Novel Companion* is designed to be used in conjunction with *Glencoe Literature*, it can easily be used independently. For example, students may wish to delay beginning their novels until after they've finished their unit work in *Glencoe Literature*. (Note that the literary elements paired with a novel draw from literary elements taught in units up to and including the unit to which the novel has been assigned, whereas the Big Ideas and reading strategies draw only from the unit to which the novel has been assigned.)

Connection to Glencoe's Literature Library

Students may use any published version of the novel in their work with the *Novel Companion*. Library editions of the titles are offered by Glencoe in its *Literature Library* series. These editions include related readings, for which the *Novel Companion* offers activities that give students the opportunity to relate themes and concepts from the novel to other types of literature.

Overview of the Structure of the *Novel Companion*

The *Novel Companion* has students practice applying advanced-level skills, first taught in *Glencoe Literature*, to excerpts from novels and other longer works. The workbook begins by introducing each novel and its author. It then breaks down the literary work into sets consisting of several chapters each. The teaching apparatus for the chapter sets mirrors that for the literature selections in *Glencoe Literature*: each has an assigned literary element, a reading strategy, accompanying vocabulary words, and writing and extension activities. Students study the literary element, reading strategy, and the Big Idea as reflected in the excerpts.

The *Novel Companion* includes two general types of lessons:

• **Interactive Reading Lessons** are lessons based on the sequential chapter groupings (chapter sets) in each novel. In this part of the workbook, students practice identifying important ideas and themes, analyzing literary elements, applying reading strategies, completing graphic organizers, and mastering vocabulary—all skills that expert readers use to help them comprehend novels and other lengthy works of literature. (See pages 4–5.)

• **Note-Taking Lessons** present two methods of note-taking to help students connect the major themes in *Glencoe Literature* to the novels and other works they will be reading. Learning these valuable methods will help students take effective notes whenever they study. (See pages 6–7.)

For an annotated outline of the *Novel Companion* structure, see pages 8–9.

Interacting with Excerpts

For each novel, students interact with 9–15 excerpts, each one or two pages long. The excerpts allow students to use targeted skills to work with targeted text. These targeted skills include 1) analyzing and evaluating literary elements inherent in the text, 2) applying advanced-level reading strategies, and 3) utilizing specialized methods of note-taking.

Interacting with Excerpts: Literary Elements
Great works of literature are ideal for studying the application of literary techniques, such as satire, and literary devices, such as hyperbole, as well as for identifying literary elements, such as diction. In both *Glencoe Literature* and the *Novel Companion*, literary techniques, devices, and elements are all referred to as *literary elements* because they are present in the literature and help to define the literature and create effects. In the *Novel Companion*, students study the particular literary elements of an excerpt by answering two literary element questions that address specific highlighted sections of that excerpt. (See page 4.)

Interacting with Excerpts: Reading Strategies Literary works are sometimes difficult to read and understand, even for advanced-level students. To help students read such works more easily and effectively, the *Novel Companion* re-teaches certain reading strategies already taught in *Glencoe Literature*. The specific strategies are determined by the complexity of the literature as well as by whether the literary elements require a review of certain reading strategies. For example, to help students understand an author's style, it may be necessary to first teach how to recognize and analyze an author's style *as you read*. Just as with the literary elements lessons, students study and apply particular reading strategies to an excerpt by answering two questions that address specific highlighted sections of that excerpt. (See page 4.)

Interacting with Excerpts: Note-Taking To help students retain what they have read, the *Novel Companion* introduces two note-taking systems and demonstrates the value of these systems by applying them to targeted areas of literary study: the study of themes and concepts. These themes and concepts appear in the form of Big Ideas

that occur in each unit of *Glencoe Literature*. By applying both note-taking approaches to a specific excerpt, students get the most out of what they've read. (See page 7).

Using Excerpts to Compare and Contrast

In addition to including excerpts from novels and other longer works, the *Novel Companion* also includes excerpts from selections that appear in *Glencoe Literature*. Students compare and contrast three or four of the longer work's literary elements with those of the *Glencoe Literature* excerpt.

Interactive Reading Lessons

The questions that appear in the interactive reading lessons help direct students through the process of reading and extracting meaning from the excerpts. The diagrams on the following pages also appear on pages 2–3 of the *Novel Companion's* student edition and serve to introduce students to these types of lessons. You may wish to review that section of the student edition with your students before having them work on the *Novel Companion*.

Get Set to Read

After reading about the novel and the author, you will begin to read the novel. You will study it in groupings of chapters, or chapter sets, in the *Novel Companion.* Each chapter set begins with an activity to connect your personal experience to the literature. You will also read background material to provide context for the chapter set content.

You're invited to interact with the information in Build Background by summarizing content or writing a caption for an image related to the content.

You are then introduced to the targeted skills for the chapter set: the Big Idea, the literary element, and the reading skill or strategy. You will also get vocabulary for the chapter set.

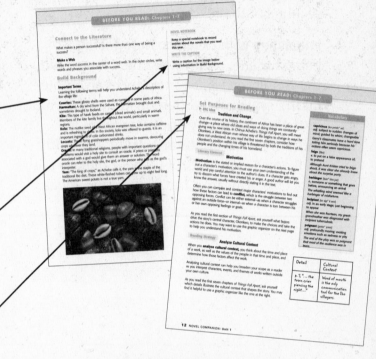

Read, Respond, Interpret

Every lesson includes an active reading graphic organizer to fill in as you read. This graphic organizer is related to either the literary element or the reading skill or strategy for the chapter set.

Interactive reading pages include text excerpts from the novels that emphasize a literary element or a reading strategy. Questions in the margin help you interact with highlighted portions of the text.

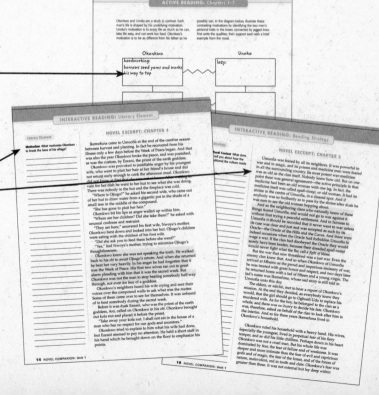

Show What You Know

After you read the chapters in the chapter set, you will answer questions about the content, including how the background information helped you as you read.

You will then demonstrate what you learned from your interactive reading of the excerpts. You will also practice using the vocabulary words you were introduced to and learn a new vocabulary word that can be used in your academic writing.

In addition, you will complete a short writing assignment and other activities related to what you read in the chapter set content. These activities will draw on what you studied in your interactive work on the excerpts from the chapters.

After you read the entire novel, you will work with related readings, connect the novel to an excerpt from *Glencoe Literature,* and finally, write an essay or story that draws upon what you learned by reading.

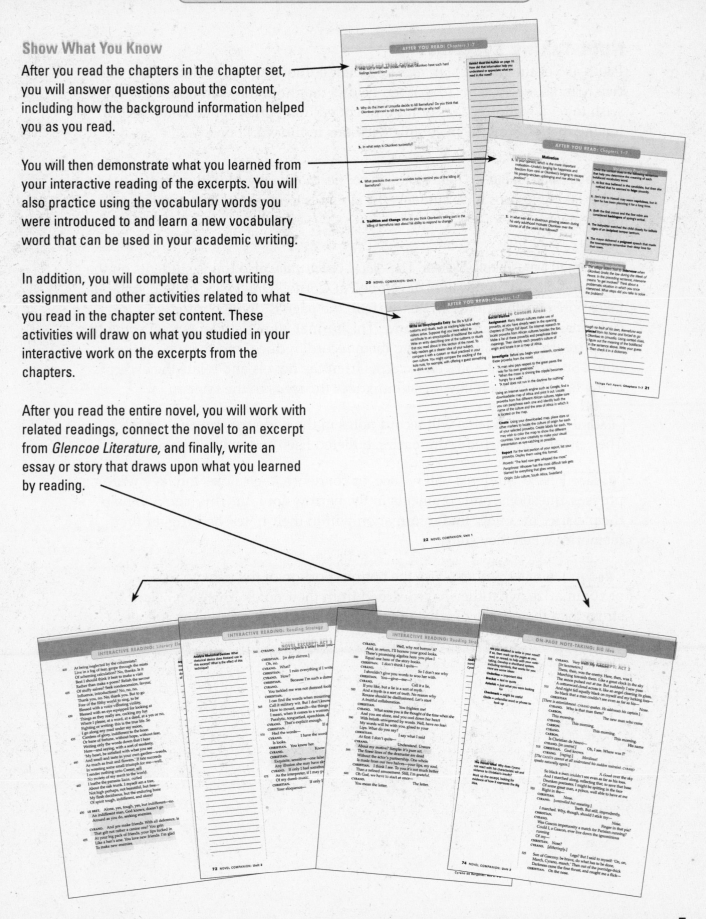

Note-Taking Systems

Pages 4–5 of the *Novel Companion's* student edition introduce students to the two note-taking systems (described below) taught in the workbook. You may wish to review those pages of the student edition with your students before having them having them complete lessons in the workbook.

On-Page Note-Taking To help students connect to the Big Idea, the On-Page Note-Taking lessons have students use symbols to mark up an excerpt directly on the page.

The Cornell Note-Taking System The *Novel Companion* also trains students on the Cornell Note-Taking System, developed at Cornell University to help students take more effective notes. In this system, the page is divided into two columns, one wide and one narrow. This format allows students to effectively organize their thinking by having them record, reduce, and then recap their notes. Students take notes on excerpts from the novels and relate the excerpts to the Big Idea. The following summarizes the steps of the system:

(Record) First, students will record notes in the wide column as they read. Their notes may include summaries, bulleted lists, and graphic organizers.

(Reduce) Next, students will reduce, or condense, their notes into key words, phrases, questions, and comments in the narrow column. This step will help them clarify meaning, find information within their notes, and trigger their memories when they study.

(Recap) Finally, students use the bottom portion of the page to recap, or summarize, what they have learned from their notes. This step helps strengthen their grasp of what they just read before they move on to the next section of text.

Note-Taking Lessons

The *Novel Companion's* note-taking lessons teach students how to record important information in their own words, reduce the information to key words they will remember, and recap their notes in a summary. Questions and activities in pages that follow allow students to apply the information from their notes.

The information below also appears on page 6 of the *Novel Companion's* student edition and serves to introduce students to these types of lesson pages. You may wish to review that page of the student edition with your students before having them complete lessons in the workbook.

Read, Question, and Mark-Up

Not only will you be interacting with excerpts from the novels as you work with the literary elements and reading strategies assigned to a chapter set, but you will also be working with excerpts that relate to the Big Idea assigned to each chapter set.

You will take notes on the excerpt—right on the page. With practice, you will devise a short-hand system that works for you. In the meantime, you can use the suggested on-page mark-up system.

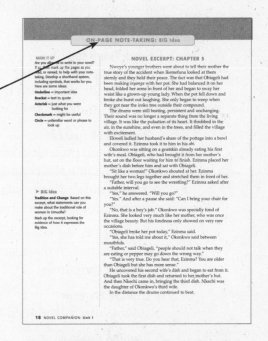

Record, Reduce, and Recap

You will also learn the Cornell Note-Taking System, described on the previous page. Here you will take notes on the excerpt you marked-up on the On-Page Note-Taking page.

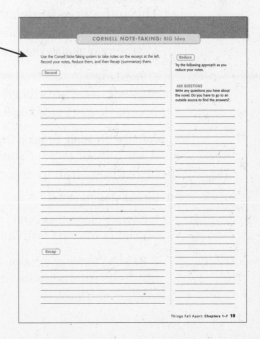

Outline of the *Novel Companion*

The following is an annotated outline of the lesson structure of the *Novel Companion*:

Novel Title Page

I. Introduction to the Novel
Students read about the novel and its place in literary history, including details about its themes and how and when it was written and published.

II. Meet the Author
Students read about the author's background and the historical, cultural, and literary context of his or her work.

III. Chapter Set

A. Before You Read

1. Connect to the Literature
Students identify with the selection in a brief activity that links the novel with the student's own experience.

2. Build Background
Students are provided with any context they will need to fully understand and appreciate the chapter set content. An accompanying activity asks students either to summarize the ideas in the background text or write a caption for a related image.

3. Big Idea
This links the chapter set content to the Big Idea that appears in the unit the novel accompanies.

4. Literary Element
Students are introduced to the targeted literary element for the chapter set.

5. Reading Strategy
This introduces students to the targeted reading strategy for the chapter set and also includes a model of a graphic organizer that students might re-create for themselves as they read.

6. Vocabulary
Students are introduced to the targeted vocabulary for the chapter. A sample sentence shows use of each word.

7. Active Reading Graphic Organizer
A graphic organizer shows students how to record literary element or reading strategy information as they read.

B. Interactive Reading

1. Literary Element excerpt
Students interact with an excerpt that relates to the targeted literary element.

2. Reading Strategy excerpt
Students interact with an excerpt that relates to the targeted reading skill or strategy.

C. Note-Taking Systems

1. Big Idea excerpt

Students interact with an excerpt that relates to the targeted Big Idea.

D. After You Read

1. Respond and Think Critically

Students answer questions about the chapter set content; at least one item addresses the Big Idea.

2. Literary Element

Students answer questions that review the targeted literary element for the chapter set.

3. Reading Strategy

Students answer questions that review the targeted reading strategy for the chapter set.

4. Vocabulary

Students review the targeted vocabulary for the chapter, using exercises that test their comprehension of the words.

5. Academic Vocabulary

Students learn a new academic vocabulary word and apply it, using an activity related to the chapter set content.

6. Writing: Personal Response, Write with Style, Write a ...

Students write in a variety of modes and produce a range of writing products as they address the content of the chapter set. In some exercises, they try out literary techniques demonstrated by the author in the chapter set.

7. Connect to Content Areas, Research and Report, Speaking and Listening

Students respond to the chapter set content through speeches, oral interpretation, research presentations, and other activities that often extend their knowledge beyond the novel itself.

IV. Work with Related Readings

Students answer questions that connect the novel with the related readings that appear in the *Literature Library* edition of the novel.

V. Connect to Other Literature

Students answer questions that connect the novel with an excerpt from another *Glencoe Literature* title.

VI. Respond Through Writing

Students write a longer piece—either narrative, persuasive, or expository—in response to the novel. The assignment guides students through the writing process, and at least one assignment in the *Novel Companion* will have students directly compare and contrast the novel to a selection in *Glencoe Literature*.

Things
Fall Apart

Chinua Achebe

Things Fall Apart *by Chinua Achebe*

One of the most influential African novels ever written, *Things Fall Apart* opened the eyes of European and American readers to traditional African life. This is exactly what Chinua Achebe set out to do. Shocked by the books about Africa he read in college—all of them by Europeans—he became determined to create an honest account of the way his people once lived and how their society was destroyed by the introduction of European commerce, religion, and law. Unusual in its form, the novel combines cultural anthropology with high drama. When *Things Fall Apart* was published in 1958, it became an immediate success. It has sold over nine million copies and has been translated into fifty-two languages.

Students at all levels can find areas of interest in *Things Fall Apart*. The novel can spark class discussions on a variety of issues, including the meaning of the word *civilization*, the responsibility for crimes against humanity, the role of women in society, the dignity of human beings, the nature of racism, and the justification for violence. *Things Fall Apart* remains one of the most thought-provoking classroom resources for a diverse society.

Synopsis

In Part One, Chinua Achebe begins the novel in a leisurely manner, introducing his readers to traditional Ibo life, including domestic and religious rituals, betrothal ceremonies, a wrestling match, a feast of locusts, a legal case, and Ibo proverbs. The protagonist is Okonkwo, a champion wrestler, warrior, and hardworking farmer, who has pulled himself up from poverty to a position of respect and leadership in the clan. Shamed by the memory of his idle father, Okonkwo is afraid of showing any sign of weakness. He treats his wives and children harshly, and when the clan's oracle calls for the death of his adopted son, Okonkwo chooses to kill the boy himself. Yet he occasionally displays tenderness, especially toward his favorite daughter, Ezinma. At the funeral of a village elder, Okonkwo accidentally kills the dead man's son when his gun explodes. He must leave Umuofia for seven years.

The plot accelerates in Parts Two and Three. Exiled to his mother's clan, Okonkwo struggles to rebuild his wealth. He learns from his friend Obierika that after members of an Ibo village killed a white man, soldiers took vengeance by wiping out the entire village. Soon Christian missionaries arrive, finding their initial converts among the outsiders of Ibo society. By the time Okonkwo returns to Umuofia, the new church has built up a thriving congregation. Justice is now administered by a District Commissioner, who ignores local customs. Enraged by the brazen disrespect of certain Christians, Okonkwo and his fellow leaders burn down the church. Fined and humiliated by the commissioner, they call a village meeting to decide on a course of action. When a court messenger arrives to break up the meeting, Okonkwo cuts off his head. Finding no support for his policy of violent resistance, he hangs himself, an action that will forever dishonor his memory.

Proverbial Wisdom

Help students understand how proverbs apply to everyday situations.

- Point out that proverbs (brief sayings that express a general truth or superstition) are found in most cultures. Invite students to give examples of proverbs, and make a list on the board.

- Divide the class into groups and ask each group to select a proverb. The group may use one from the class list or one of the following:

  – A stitch in time saves nine.

  – Don't count your chickens before they hatch.

  – Look before you leap.

  – A friend in need is a friend indeed.

  – He who laughs last laughs best.

- Ask students to create a skit exemplifying the wisdom expressed in the proverb. Other students should try to guess which proverb is being acted out.

- Point out that in cultures that lack written language, the spoken word preserves the literature, values, and history of the people. Proverbs form an important part of daily life in the Ibo world of *Things Fall Apart*.

Nobody's Perfect

Encourage students to think about the virtues and flaws that exist in every society.

- Discuss the idea of a utopia, or ideal society. Is there a general agreement on what constitutes a perfect world? Why is it that people have been unable to realize such a dream?

- Remind students that for many people, the United States represents a land of wealth, equality, and opportunity. But how far are we from being a utopia? Brainstorm with students a list of the pros and cons of American society. Discuss their ideas and identify items they consider particularly important. Does the balance sheet come out in favor of the United States?

- Point out that *Things Fall Apart* describes two societies in conflict, one similar to our own and one very different. Encourage students as they read to look for favorable and unfavorable aspects of each society.

The View from Mars

Introduce students to the idea that social customs may look strange from the outside.

- Invite students to share experiences they have had in other cultures. What customs did they observe that seemed unusual? Point out that people in all cultures conduct the everyday business of life in ways that may at first seem very unusual to outsiders.

- Ask students to imagine that they are introducing curious visitors from another planet to their way of life. Have them form pairs and choose an ordinary daily activity, such as eating lunch in the cafeteria, going to the movies, or driving a car. Ask them to think about the activity step-by-step, remembering that everything is new for their listeners.

- Invite volunteers to describe their activity as if talking to an audience of interplanetary visitors. Encourage the audience to ask about details that they did not understand.

RELATED READINGS	MAKING CONNECTIONS TO *Things Fall Apart*
The Second Coming by William Butler Yeats (Glencoe's *Literature Library,* BLM page 24)	**This poem explains the title of the novel.** <ul><li>Ask students to take a moment to jot down ways in which the world might undergo a drastic change. Discuss their suggestions. Ask them whether they would fear or welcome such changes.</li><li>Explain the biblical reference in the poem's title (referring to the second coming of Jesus Christ). Point out that Yeats's apocalyptic vision was inspired by turmoil in Europe, particularly in Ireland.</li><li>After students read the poem, have them choose lines or images they found striking or unusual. Discuss how the passages they chose contribute to the poem's overall effect and purpose.</li></ul>
Chinua Achebe: A Storyteller Far from Home by Somini Sengupta (Glencoe's *Literature Library,* BLM page 25)	**This reading will help readers understand the importance of homeland to Achebe.** <ul><li>Give students a few minutes to create a word web based on the word *home*. Have them jot down any associations they have with the concept. Take a survey of their thoughts. Are there any recurring themes?</li><li>Ask students to remember a time when they were far away from home. How did they feel? What did they miss the most? Is there a difference between being away for a set amount of time and not knowing when you will return?</li></ul>
The Gentlemen of the Jungle by Jomo Kenyatta **He Who Has Lost All** by David Diop (Glencoe's *Literature Library,* BLM page 26)	**These readings expand on themes introduced in the novel.** <ul><li>Before reading, have students consider what typically happens to a people when their country is ruled by outsiders. Why do colonized nations yearn for independence?</li><li>After reading, point out that although these selections share a point of view, they differ greatly in tone (general mood or effect). Discuss what contributes to this difference. Which selection is most similar in tone to *Things Fall Apart*?</li></ul>
from **West With the Night** by Beryl Markham (Glencoe's *Literature Library,* BLM page 27)	**This essay presents another personal view of Africa.** <ul><li>Before reading, have students brainstorm a list of ways in which people might describe the United States. Is there a single way of representing the characteristics of a place?</li><li>Explain that Beryl Markham was an Englishwoman brought up in Africa. Ask students to consider how her point of view might differ from Achebe's. Invite them to discuss the different ways in which Markham and Achebe describe the land they both consider home.</li></ul>
My Children! My Africa! by Athol Fugard (Glencoe's *Literature Library,* BLM page 28)	**Fugard's drama presents the results of colonization in another African nation.** <ul><li>Before reading, prepare students for the play's social and political context. Point out that the play is set at a time when South Africa's apartheid system was breaking up under internal and external pressure.</li><li>After reading, challenge students with the play's central question: Is violence an acceptable means of social change?</li><li>Help students look for connections between this play's context and that of *Things Fall Apart* (Africans under European domination).</li></ul>

All answers are sample answers except those for Vocabulary Practice.

CHAPTERS 1–7

BEFORE YOU READ
Write the Caption

In parts of Africa, people once used cowrie shells for money.

ACTIVE READING

hardworking: borrows seed yams and works his way to top/*lazy:* doesn't bother to prepare new land each year; *athletic:* a champion wrestler at age 18/*artistic:* loves to play his flute at festivals; *brave:* has taken five heads in battle/*cowardly:* can't bear the sight of blood; *rich:* has three wives and a barn full of yams/*poor:* always in debt and barely able to feed his family; *respected:* holds two titles/*despised:* sent to die in Evil Forest

INTERACTIVE READING
Literary Element: Motivation

His anger, built up over a lifetime, is uncontrollable and drives him to do rash things.

Literary Element: Motivation

Okonkwo has always been both very proud and fearful that he will look like a fool to others, as his father did. He doesn't trust that anyone will understand him, so he can't admit his mistakes, and he hardens himself against his people—and the world.

Reading Strategy: Analyze Cultural Context

They are highly superstitious in their beliefs and put their faith in the opinions of an oracle.

Reading Strategy: Analyze Cultural Context

Okonkwo is a rich and powerful man in the village. Because Ikemefuna was given as payment to the village, he must be cared for by someone who can afford to keep him but who will not treat him too kindly. Okonkwo is that person.

ON-PAGE NOTE-TAKING
BIG Question: Tradition and Change

Women are subservient to their husbands; each wife brings and serves a separate dish to the husband at each meal.

AFTER YOU READ
Respond and Think Critically

1. Unoka was lazy, artistic, and impractical. Okonkwo suffered hardship and humiliation as a result of his father's behavior.

2. The Oracle calls for the killing. Since Okonkwo withdraws to the rear of the line, it's likely that he does not intend to kill Ikemefuna, but when the boy runs toward him, Okonkwo feels he must strike him down to avoid being perceived as weak.

3. He is successful by the conventional standards of his people: he has physical prowess, wealth, three wives, and titles.

4. Answers may vary. Likely responses include the execution of political prisoners, gang violence, and political kidnapping.

5. Okonkwo's fear of being thought weak or wrong in any way is so strong within him that he does not listen to the elder who tells him to take no part in the killing. His inability to change something so deeply ingrained suggests that he will not respond well to changes in his society.

Apply Background

Answers will vary. Students may mention Achebe's quote about wanting to show the world that Africans are people, not savages. They may say that the chapter set reveals Okonkwo to be a deeply flawed but also deeply human character.

Literary Element: Motivation

1. Answers may vary. Some students may feel that the quest for happiness is a strong spiritual guideline. Others may believe that hard work and tenacity are the way to achieve a good life.

2. Okonkwo survived the hardship of a rainy season when everything went wrong for him. He used this as a marker of all the bad that happens in the world. It made a survivor of him and motivated him to work against any odds to rise above his circumstances.

Reading Strategy: Analyze Cultural Context

1. Students may mention the deal that Umuofia strikes with the Mbaino, which brings Ikemefuna to Okonkwo's home. They may also mention the way the villagers in Umuofia discuss the practices of other clans and villages as a way of thinking about their own practices in such matters. For example,

the custom in Obodoani is that anyone who breaks the peace during Peace Week is killed by the village. Okonkwo's village understands this but finds it too harsh a punishment for their own practices.

2. The kola nut is brought out when business deals are being discussed, when friends and family come to visit, and in other social situations. It seems to be an offering of welcome or friendship. Allowing another person to break the kola nut is a mark of mutual respect or goodwill.

Vocabulary Practice

1. The words *believed* and *but then* make it clear that Ana changed her mind. The inference is that the candidate was only pretending to be sincere.

2. The sentence is constructed in such a way that "planning it for a long time" is an antonym for *capricious*.

3. The words "first" and "spring's arrival" give clues to the meaning.

4. The words "telltale signs" show that the tantrum is not yet in full swing; therefore one can assume it might be just beginning.

5. Anything that makes people remember their deep love must be profoundly moving.

Academic Vocabulary

1. Answers will vary. Students should exhibit understanding of the word by describing a situation in which they stepped in to settle a conflict or other problem.

2. The words "forced to go with Okonkwo" provide clues that *displaced* means "relocated."

Writing

Write an Encyclopedia Entry

Students' may select from any number of Ibo traditional behaviors, including

• the punishment for domestic crimes, such as Okonkwo's beating of his wife

• the care of foster children

• the payment of debts

Research and Report

Literary Criticism

Students should be evaluated on both the visual and textual components of their reports. The visuals should be clear and eye-catching. The text should be concise and well written. Both components should work together to form a cohesive project presented using performance techniques such as modulated voice, good posture, and eye contact.

CHAPTERS 8–13

BEFORE YOU READ
Summarize

The Ibo people are deeply connected, in their religious ceremonies and their daily lives, to the spirit world, which is inhabited by their ancestors.

ACTIVE READING

reckless: defends the killing of Ikemefuna in an argument with Obierika; threatens to beat Ezinma if she doesn't locate her *iyi-uwa*; fires his defective gun during Ezeudu's funeral, killing the dead man's son

caring: deeply affected by Ikemefuna's death—doesn't eat for two days; follows Ezinma to the Oracle's cave to make sure that she is safe; works hard to cure Ezinma

INTERACTIVE READING

Literary Element: Anthropomorphism

Gluttony and lying lead to a bad end. Cunning and manipulation are despised in Ibo culture and deserve punishment.

Literary Element: Anthropomorphism

The folktale explains how the tortoise got its variegated shell. The story might also be a way to explain the temporary disappearance of birds due to migratory flight habits.

Reading Strategy: Make Inferences About Characters

Ekwefi trusts other women to be sympathetic to the idea of protecting a child, but she believes Chielo to be more spirit than woman at this point.

Reading Strategy: Make Inferences About Characters

Okonkwo followed Ekwefi to make sure she and Ezinma would be safe. He is far too proud to let Ekwefi know this, but she knows it just the same.

ON-PAGE NOTE-TAKING
BIG Idea: Tradition and Change

Most of the people believe themselves to be governed by the spirits of their ancestors, the *egwugwu,* but in fact the *egwugwu* are actually powerful men of the clan disguised in special costumes. So the clan is actually self-governed.

AFTER YOU READ
Respond and Think Critically

1. She is his favorite child. She understands him well, he feels comfortable expressing his affection to her, and she resembles her mother.

2. Chielo has carried Ezinma around the villages and into the cave. The incident reveals that Okonkwo is more concerned about Ezinma than he is willing to let on and that he still has affection and love for Ekwefi.

3. He must go into exile for seven years, and his compound is completely destroyed. Killing a member of one's own clan is very serious, but Okonkwo does not receive the harshest punishment because he didn't intend to kill the boy.

4. Okonkwo would be very likely be sentenced to prison. Students may or may not feel imprisonment would be a fairer punishment.

5. Answers will vary. Students may mention such elements as the groom's clan bringing a certain number of pots of wine and the bride's mother having to cook for the entire village.

Apply Background

Students may respond that a great deal of this chapter set has to do with the spiritual life of the Ibo clan, including a legal proceeding in which the ancestral spirits appeared in elaborate costumes and masks.

Literary Element: Anthropomorphism

1. She told a story attributing the human characteristic of unrequited love to the mosquito and the ear in order to explain this common occurrence.

2. They say the moon is refusing food and pouting.

Reading Strategy: Make Inferences About Characters

1. The company of men sitting around talking and drinking palm wine gives him a sense of comfort and familiarity, and takes his mind off his troubles. He is able to justify his taking part in Ikemefuna's killing because he once again feels secure in his place in the village.

2. She still cares very deeply for Okonkwo.

Vocabulary Practice

1. B, 2. B, 3. B, 4. A, 5. A

Academic Vocabulary

1. Answers will vary. Students might identify aspects of their religious faith, their code of ethics, or their beliefs about friendship or family.

2. Definition: to disagree with; synonyms: challenge, deny; antonyms: correspond, to agree with; sentence: I have to contradict a person who tells lies about someone else.

Writing
Personal Response

Answers will vary.

Speaking and Listening
Interview

Students' interviews should be based on clear and well-written questions. Their reports should integrate three different sets of interviewees' quotes as well as descriptions of events and ideas from the novel.

CHAPTERS 14–25

BEFORE YOU READ
Summarize

When Europeans tried to impose their culture on Africans, a clash of cultures was inevitable. David Livingstone, traveled to Africa as a missionary, but he later took up the fight against African slave trade.

ACTIVE READING

Attributes of the tragic hero: physically imposing; respected in his society; doomed by a personal flaw.

Ways in which Okonknwo shows these attributes: champion wrestler, brave in battle; prosperous farmer, has three wives and many children; when Europeans take over many aspect of his culture, he can neither reverse nor tolerate changes and is destroyed by his inflexibility.

INTERACTIVE READING

Literary Element: Archetype

The idea of virginity and purity of the bride before marriage is a theme archetype based on traditional beliefs in many societies throughout the world.

Literary Element: Archetype

The character archetype is the protective mother. Sample paraphrase: If you want to respect the spirit of your mother, be grateful for the many good things you have been given here in her homeland.

Reading Strategy: Analyze Style

The story Obierika tells is horrifying—all the more so because it is told in very simple terms. Obierika reveals no emotion, which allows the terror and sadness of the events to speak for themselves.

Reading Strategy: Analyze Style

The author ends the chapter with a small joke between the men; the scene so far has been very tense, and the author's intention at this point is probably to provide a bit of comic relief. The tone is light hearted but sincere.

ON-PAGE NOTE-TAKING

BIG Idea: The Price of Freedom

The missionaries divide the Ibo people from one another when some members of Okonkwo's community convert to Christianity. These converts persuade others to join the church as well. Eventually Umuofia is divided into two groups—those who believe in Christianity and those who stay with their traditional beliefs. Because the clan is divided in its ideology, there are fewer people to stand up for the old ways. This enables the whites to install a government, courts, and schools.

AFTER YOU READ

Respond and Think Critically

1. Nwoye is attracted by the hymns and the way Christianity includes people rejected by traditional Ibo religion. Okonkwo disinherits Nwoye for breaking with tradition and for not behaving in a "manly" way.

2. Mr. Brown is tolerant, curious, and diplomatic. Mr. Smith is intolerant, zealous, and rash. Under Mr. Brown, the Christians avoid open conflict with the traditional Ibo, but Mr. Smith allows his followers to offend and anger them.

3. Some students may suggest that Okonkwo's act was done out of pure anger, that it is futile because it is already too late to change the course of the village's fate. Others may argue that Okonkwo's action shows courage and commitment.

4. Some students may suggest that Nwoye would be ashamed of the way his father died. Others might respond that Nwoye's sensitive nature could cause him to resent the District Commissioner's harsh treatment of the Ibo.

5. They meet to decide what action to take after their leaders have been imprisoned. Court messengers arrive to break up the meeting, and Okonkwo kills the head messenger. The people of Umuofia are too divided and fearful to go to war.

Apply Background

Answers will vary. Students may say that the information about David Livingstone gave them some perspective on the differences between Mr. Brown and Mr. Smith in the novel.

Literary Element: Archetype

1. Okonkwo has a very strict image of what makes an Ibo man. He tries to live according to that image, but the world changes around him, making his quest all but impossible. In the end, he chooses to destroy himself rather than live in a world where his self-image cannot remain intact.

2. Smith sees the archetype of black as evil and white as good. To his mind, he must convert the Ibo people because their ways are inherently evil.

Reading Strategy: Analyze Style

1. The repetition illustrates the gradual deterioration of the Ibo people's unity.

Vocabulary Practice

1. same
2. opposite
3. same
4. opposite
5. opposite

Academic Vocabulary

1. The word *connections* suggests a meeting of minds. *Migrate* means "to drift or move toward."

2. Answers will vary. Students may list boredom, anger, degree of difficulty, growing up, or other factors.

Write with Style

Apply Tone

Students should use an interesting or entertaining event from their own lives as the basis for their paragraph. Encourage them to understand that the detached narrative style does not mean that the story should lack detail or interesting ideas.

Speaking and Listening

Speech

Students' presentations should be oriented toward a specific point of view about how to solve the problem of the white missionaries' treatment of the men of Umuofia. The speech should include at least one rhetorical question. Watch for strong presentation techniques involving eye contact, vocal quality and projection, and posture.

WORK WITH RELATED READINGS

On *Things Fall Apart*

Possible answers: Ibo society falls apart under the pressure of British colonialism; Achebe's novel, like Yeats's poem, portrays a transition from one era to another.

Chinua Achebe: A Storyteller Far from Home

They both feel unhappy, powerless, and unmotivated in their new lands, and both long to return home despite the friendly welcome they receive.

The Gentlemen of the Jungle
He Who Has Lost All

Some students might say that the man in the story reminds them of Okonkwo because he takes violent action against his oppressors. Others might respond that the bitterness of the poem's speaker reminds them of Okonkwo.

from West With the Night

Students may suggest that Achebe's characters do live more closely in tune with elemental forces than people from industrial nations; others may think that the characters have much in common with people everywhere.

My Children! My Africa!

Okonkwo and Mr. M hold completely opposite views on whether to use violence to confront injustice. However, both men cling to old-fashioned beliefs, and they both die because they have become alienated from their people.

CONNECT TO OTHER LITERATURE

Character In some ways Okonkwo and the panther have a lot in common. Each feels trapped—the panther by its bars and cage, Okonkwo by his circumstances in life and by the arrival of the white missionaries who change his way of life. However, while the panther paces endlessly, Okonkwo decides to end his own life.

Archetype They are similar archetypes. Okonkwo is a noted warrior and wrestler who is both respected and feared. The panther is cunning and fierce, an excellent hunter in the wild. Okonkwo is undone by his pride, his temper, and his inability to change. His actions and circumstances lead him to kill himself rather than live under the whites' rule. The panther has no such choice; it cannot change its fate and must bear its loss of freedom in silence and solitude.

Tone Achebe's tone resembles oral storytelling; it is detached, neither commending nor condemning Okonkwo's actions. Rilke's tone makes it clear that he sympathizes with the plight of the caged panther.

Write About It

Both subjects feel loss and confusion. Students' responses to the idea of loss of freedom will vary.

RESPOND THROUGH WRITING

Persuasive Essay

Students' persuasive essays should use logic and reasoning to persuade the reader of the negative or positive aspects of missionaries working in foreign lands. Ask students to include their charts along with their written reports. Charts should contain both arguments that support the student's point of view and counterarguments that refute it.

Cyrano de Bergerac

Edmond Rostand

Cyrano de Bergerac *by Edmond Rostand*

Cyrano de Bergerac was one of the nineteenth century's greatest dramatic successes. The play's success rests mostly with its larger-than-life hero, a swashbuckling poet with a sensitive heart that isn't reflected by his physically unappealing exterior. Cyrano's wit, passion, idealism, bravery, and integrity, not to mention his colossal nose, continue to captivate audiences today.

Synopsis

The play opens at a theater, where a pompous actor, Montfleury, is about to perform. Cyrano de Bergerac, a well-known poet-soldier from the southwestern province of Gascony, has warned Montfleury not to perform and drives the actor from the stage. Afterward, Cyrano tells his friend Le Bret about his long and secret love for his cousin Roxane. Although Le Bret urges Cyrano to speak to her about his love, Cyrano bitterly refuses because he is ashamed of his long nose. Roxane, however, has fallen in love with a new member of Cyrano's company, Christian, and wishes Cyrano to protect him from harm. Cyrano reluctantly agrees. Christian is revealed to be a handsome and brave young soldier who lacks the wit and cleverness to captivate Roxane. Cyrano offers to compose love letters for the young soldier to help him woo Roxane.

Cyrano's military commander de Guiche, who is a rival for Roxane's heart as well as an enemy of Cyrano's, threatens to send the company to war. Cleverly, Roxane convinces de Guiche that keeping the company from going into battle will infuriate Cyrano, who longs for glory.

De Guiche agrees, not realizing that Roxane's true intention is to keep Christian safe from harm. Roxane tricks a monk into marrying her and Christian. When de Guiche learns what has happened, he is furious. In retaliation, he orders the company to the front.

Unexpectedly, Roxane arrives at the camp. She explains to Christian that she realizes she loves him not for his outward appearance but for his inward beauty. Christian forces Cyrano to admit that he, too, loves Roxane and urges Cyrano to reveal the sham. But before Christian can set the revelation in motion, he is mortally wounded. Cyrano places a letter he wrote to Roxane in Christian's hands so that she may find it there as Christian's last words to her.

The final scene takes place fifteen years later. Roxane lives in a convent, where she has retired to mourn Christian's death and cherish his memory. Cyrano visits her faithfully. On the day of his last visit to Roxane, he is struck by a falling log in the street, probably dropped by one of his numerous enemies, and is dying. He asks to read Christian's final letter to Roxane, which she keeps with her at all times. Although it is now too dark to read, he recites the words by heart. Hearing this, Roxane suddenly realizes that Cyrano has been her true love all these years and belatedly confesses her love for him. Cyrano, however, is dying. In his final words, he proudly claims that although everything is gone, one thing, his panache, remains unsullied in death.

Skin Deep

Have students examine ways in which physical appearance affects personal judgments.

- Write on the chalkboard the well-known aphorism "You can't judge a book by its cover." Ask students to explain the meaning of the phrase.

- Have students decide whether they agree with the phrase. Then ask if there are any circumstances in which they believe people can make judgments based on appearance alone. Ask them to describe such situations. Then discuss how physical beauty can influence the judgments we make about people.

- Have students examine the dangers of judging people by their appearance. If appropriate, have volunteers describe situations in which they made mistaken judgments based on appearance alone.

- Conclude the activity by explaining that one of the themes of the play they are about to read is the relationship of physical beauty to inner beauty.

Vive la France!

Have students synthesize prior knowledge about French culture, society, and history.

- Draw a word web on the board, with the word *France* at the center.

- Ask students to help you complete the web with information about France. You may want to get them started with a few ideas of your own.

- As students suggest words relevant to French culture, society, and history, have them explain the particular significance of each word and the source from which they learned it.

- Conclude the activity by explaining that *Cyrano de Bergerac* is one of the most popular plays written by a French author and that it portrays an especially colorful era in the nation's history.

Verve

Help students understand the concept of *panache*.

- Ask students if they can define *panache*. If not, write this definition on the chalkboard: "a special style, flair, dash, or verve that distinguishes a person." A person with panache usually has a dashing or flamboyant manner.

- Explain that the literal meaning of the word is "plume." Ask why the word for a jaunty, waving cluster of feathers on a hat or helmet might have taken on its second meaning.

- Have students name people they feel possess panache and explain why. List the people on the chalkboard. Examples might include celebrities, friends, or relatives.

- End by saying that the hero of the play they are about to read is one of literature's greatest examples of someone who possesses panache. Ask them to note words and actions that have earned the hero this reputation.

RELATED READINGS	MAKING CONNECTIONS TO *Cyrano de Bergerac*
The Masterpieces from *Edmond Rostand* by Alba della Fazia Amoia (Glencoe's *Literature Library,* BLM page 33)	**In this discussion of Rostand and his masterpiece, the author refers to Cyrano as a heroic figure who "loves sincerity and courage above all."** • Have students brainstorm a list of modern-day people who might be called heroes. List names on the board. • Have students work in small groups or in pairs, and give them ten minutes to write a list of heroic qualities or personality traits. Read aloud the dictionary definition of *hero*. Have groups rework their lists of qualities as needed to correspond to the dictionary definition. • Have students use their lists of heroic traits to discuss the people they listed earlier as heroes. Who still qualifies? Have new names come to mind?
"Cyrano de Bergerac" and "Cyrano" in English by Max Beerbohm (Glencoe's *Literature Library,* BLM page 34)	**Max Beerbohm had been the drama critic for London's *Saturday Review* for only one month when he was given the assignment to review the original Paris production of *Cyrano de Bergerac*. The play had just opened in London.** • Ask for volunteers to choose a movie they have seen recently to review for the class. • After students listen to one or more reviews, work with them to create a list of criteria they would use to review a movie.
Beauty: When the Other Dancer Is the Self by Alice Walker (Glencoe's *Literature Library,* BLM page 35)	**Alice Walker says she spent many years of her life believing that a scar on her eye made her unattractive.** • Have students discuss, in small or large groups, where we get our ideas of beauty (TV, movies, family, friends). Are these ideas realistic? • Discuss with students whether standards of beauty vary from place to place or over time. (You might show the class pictures of "beautiful people" from non-European cultures or from the past.) • Conclude by having students write about the most beautiful person they know and why he or she is beautiful.

On Falling in Love
 by Robert Louis Stevenson
 (Glencoe's *Literature Library,* BLM page 36)
	Love interests everyone, for better or for worse.
	 • Have students discuss the following quotations.
	   – "All's fair in love and war." (Smedley, *Frank Fairleigh*)
	   – "'Tis better to have loved and lost than never to have loved at all." (Tennyson: "In Memoriam A. H. H." canto 27)
	   – "To do good and communicate is the lover's grand intention. It is the happiness of the other that makes his own most intense gratification." (Stevenson: "On Falling in Love")

Strangers in Love by Esther Gwinnell (Glencoe's *Literature Library,* BLM page 37)	**According to Dr. Esther Gwinnell, letter writing, although not as popular as it used to be, can often provide rich and deep communication.** • Ask students when they might write a note instead of using a phone or e-mail. • List on the board the advantages of writing a letter instead of phoning, texting, or e-mailing. • If students have read "Strangers in Love," have them list the advantages the author discusses.

All answers are sample answers except those for Vocabulary Practice.

ACT 1

BEFORE YOU READ
Write the Caption

French playwright Moliere wrote comedies in verse in the seventeenth century that served as a model for *Cyrano de Bergerac.*

ACTIVE READING

- He is brave but also clever because he knows people are brave in a group but not individually.

- He is a man of artistic sophistication.

- He enjoys making grand gestures but also is fair.

- He is extremely sensitive about his nose.

- He is very clever with words.

- He is a great poet as well as a masterful fencer.

- He is courteous and does not want to deprive the poor foodseller of her livelihood.

- He likes to be "on center stage" but has another, hidden side to his personality.

- He has an inferiority complex about his appearance and does not believe that Roxane could love him for his inner worth.

- He loves the chance to achieve a spectacular success in front of all Paris, as well as to defend a poet.

INTERACTIVE READING
Literary Element: Hero

The heroic ideal is exemplified by a person who is brave and fearless but is also well rounded and excels at a wide number of pursuits. By defending the theater, Cyrano shows his appreciation for the arts; through his speech, he shows that he is a poet and an orator, and by taking on the opposition, he shows that he is fearless.

Literary Element: Hero

Answers may vary. Students may say that because Cyrano proves himself both a swordsman and a poet, his confidence is well earned, which makes him heroic. Others may say that Cyrano's acting upon his opinion of Montfleury's lack of artistic skill is not heroic, since

Montfleury's shortcomings are not enough to justify stopping a performance, let alone fighting a duel to the death.

Reading Strategy: Identify Genre

Cyrano is very witty and fires off one-liners even as he duels with Valvert. Valvert is bested both at verbal skill and swordsmanship, much to his frustration.

Reading Strategy: Identify Genre

Cyrano kills Valvert.

ON-PAGE NOTE-TAKING
BIG Idea: The Heroic Ideal

Cyrano is by their account a poet, a fighter, a doctor, and a musician—all qualities that might contribute to the heroic ideal.

AFTER YOU READ
Respond and Think Critically

1. Cyrano will cut them in half with his sword. He is very sensitive about his appearance and has a lethal temper.

2. Valvert calls him a poet by referring to his "doggerel recital." Cyrano composes a poem while fighting the viscount.

3. Le Bret tells Cyrano to declare his love for Roxane. Cyrano rejects the advice because he is afraid Roxane will spurn his love and laugh at his nose.

4. He is unhinged by her—his knees knock and he falls in love instantly. He is somewhat innocent and not very worldly. He is not gifted verbally and he is often struck speechless.

5. Some students may respond that Cyrano has a worthy goal. Others may note that perfectionists can never be satisfied with their own and others' achievements.

Apply Background

Students may cite the introduction's mention of the play's witty use of language, its lack of naturalism, and Rostand's respect and love for the theater as elements that helped them interpret the events in Act 1.

Literary Element: Hero

1. Cyrano is self-conscious about his appearance. He feels his nose makes him unlovable to women. He shuts himself off from a chance of happiness with his belief that he is not worthy.

2. He is aggressive and fights with and insults anyone who looks at him for too long or makes an offhand comment about his nose.

Reading Strategy: Identify Genre

1. It is a comic scene. As he duels, Cyrano improvises a complicated verse ballad with a rhyme scheme of ababbcbc.

2. Students may say that Cyrano's mentioning the world as a theater and life as a play adds both poetry and comedy to the end of the act.

Vocabulary Practice

1. bellicose
2. lambast
3. cynosure
4. affable
5. enmity

Academic Vocabulary

1. Students' examples will vary, but the idea should be that biases can be either positive or negative depending on whether they engender action in a negative or a positive direction.

2. definition: lie beneath; synonyms: motivate, cause, trigger; antonyms: encompass; sentence: Foolishness can underlie even the most noble-sounding plans.

Write with Style

Apply Form

Students' monologues should be evaluated on creativity as well as adherence to the guidelines. Encourage them to use interesting word combinations.

Speaking and Listening

Oral Interpretation

Have students hand in their marked-up monologues after the presentation. Their presentations should reveal an understanding of the events leading up to the monologue in the play, the character's emotions, and the action surrounding the character.

ACT 2

BEFORE YOU READ

Summarize

The Three Musketeers is one example of the swashbuckler genre.

ACTIVE READING

Possible answers: Cyrano and Le Bret: Cyrano wins, arguing that it is better to be alone, free to make enemies, than to be the darling of a corrupt society. Christian and Cyrano: either one could be seen as the winner—Cyrano because he know the collaboration

will make Roxane happy for a while and allow him to express his love, Christian because he knows the deceit is bound to be discovered in the end.

INTERACTIVE READING

Literary Element: Argument

Students' responses to Cyrano's argument will vary, but they should back up their opinions with ideas from the play.

Literary Element: Argument

Le Bret's argument is that though Cyrano claims indifference, an indifferent man doesn't go out of his way to make enemies of people the way Cyrano does. Cyrano compares Le Bret's friendships to the slavish devotion of dogs.

Reading Strategy: Analyze Rhetorical Devices

The playwright uses repetition to emphasize both the similarities and the differences in Christian's and Cyrano's points of view about Roxane.

Reading Strategy: Analyze Rhetorical Devices

It is ironic that Cyrano would make such an appeal because he loves Roxane himself. His reasoning is that he will be wooing her on some level, but the fact that he is doing it in the name of another man is pure literary irony.

ON-PAGE NOTE-TAKING

BIG Idea: The Heroic Ideal

He has made a vow to Roxane to protect the young soldier. He cannot break this vow—he is far too devoted to Roxane to allow himself to do that—but he is also impressed with Christian's bravery.

AFTER YOU READ

Respond and Think Critically

1. When she says the man she loves is handsome. It shows that Cyrano believes Roxane can never love him because of his physical ugliness.

2. Christian insults Cyrano's nose to prove his bravery to the other cadets. Cyrano suppresses his anger. He values his promise to Roxane and will keep his word.

3. Cyrano will give Christian the words to woo Roxane. He may genuinely want to help the two lovers, or he may feel it is a chance to share his own feelings about her.

4. Answers will vary. Students may note that Cyrano just assumes Roxane is talking about him when she talks about her love, he refuses to join de Guiche's retinue, he refuses payment for his poems, and he boasts of the way he battled 100 men. Students may

also note that legitimate self-confidence does not typically lead people into dangerous or foolhardy situations they cannot handle.

5. Students who feel his actions are believable may cite his strong sense of honor, his devotion to Roxane, or his firm belief that she could never love him. Students who feel his actions are not believable may claim that jealousy is inevitable in such a situation and that rivalry would prevent most people from performing such a selfless task. Sense of honor, devotion, and loyalty are all aspects of the heroic ideal.

Apply Background

Students should note that Cyrano's recklessness and daring as well as his virtuous treatment of Roxane and Christian are aspects of the swashbuckler genre.

Literary Element: Argument

1. Roxane wants to use their shared past as leverage for Cyrano to do her the favor of protecting her love interest. Cyrano on the other hand, wants to use their old familiarity as the basis for a declaration of love between them.

2. Answers will vary. Some students may say that Cyrano's obvious love for Roxane provides the more persuasive argument. Others will say that because Roxane gets Cyrano to do what she wants him to do, she clearly has the more persuasive argument.

Reading Strategy: Rhetorical Devices

1. Students should note Cyrano's repetition of "Ah," Roxane's emotional appeal to him to protect Christian, and connotative words such as *beautiful,* which is what makes Cyrano suddenly realize Roxane is not referring to him as the man she loves.

2. The playwright uses repetition to show that the cadets are both bragging and joking about their high-born backgrounds ("Baron," "Barons," "Baronially born"). This builds expectation and comedy, culminating in the second cadet's admission that all the barons have hocked their baronial crowns.

Vocabulary Practice

1. a
2. g
3. f
4. d
5. b

Academic Vocabulary

1. In the second sentence, *equipped* means "outfitted" or "operational." *Equipped* in the first context means "to be endowed with personal qualities." *Equipped* in the second context means "set up with tools or equipment."

2. The word *only* makes it clear that *reinforces* does not contradict but rather strengthens the idea. Therefore *reinforces* means "makes stronger."

Write with Style
Apply Parallel Sentence Structure

Students' paragraphs should

- show clear understanding of parallel sentence structure
- use at least two sentences that display parallel sentence structure
- use vibrant word choices

Speaking and Listening
Literature Groups

Students' group activity should be evaluated in terms of the clarity of the examples used, the cohesion of the collective presentation, and the individual contribution of each member.

ACT 3

BEFORE YOU READ
Summarize

The real Cyrano, like his fictional counterpart, was a great duelist, writer, and speaker who coached others in these arts; he also happened to have a very long nose.

ACTIVE READING

Possible answers: Touch: "I shall take all words that ever were . . . mad armfuls, not bouquets, I'll smother you in them." Smell: "perfumed velvet wraps us close." Taste: "the sweetest word, the ultimate honey, stings like vinegar." Emotional responses will vary.

INTERACTIVE READING
Literary Element: Imagery

Sight: *heavy with honey, clogs of accident and decay, cloak of trailing blackness, I am shadow, sunlit through darkness, white gown of summer; its wings a haze of love; it zigzags to the orifice of your tiny ear and buzzes*
Touch: *crushing my heart like a stone, a choking asthma, plucking flowers*
Smell: *sweetness in all the flowers of the earth, a heap of rose petals*

Literary Element: Imagery

She is cautious. Up until now, she has not been in love with Christian's words—only his appearance. As she hears this new language from him, full of emotion and poetry, she is hesitant but begins to fall in love with the other side of him, not knowing of course that it is Cyrano whose words she truly loves.

Reading Strategy: Make and Verify Predictions About Plot

Answers will vary. Students will likely predict that De Guiche will try to seek revenge on Cyrano, Christian, or Roxane. They may base their predictions on the fact that De Guiche has already revealed himself to be a small-minded and untrustworthy character.

Reading Strategy: Make and Verify Predictions About Plot

Cyrano will write the letters for Christian. He has served as Christian's poetic voice to this point and is most likely to continue.

ON-PAGE NOTE-TAKING

BIG Idea: The Heroic Ideal

Acting out of the heroic ideals of passion and loyalty, Cyrano celebrates both the pleasure and the pain of his love by distracting de Guiche until the marriage between Roxane and Christian has taken place. He speaks skillfully and displays great intellectual ability, which are also traits of the heroic ideal.

AFTER YOU READ

Respond and Think Critically

1. She is concerned because Christian will be in danger. She tricks de Guiche by persuading him that staying home from the war will infuriate Cyrano. She is an articulate, quick-thinking person, which is part of the reason Cyrano loves her.

2. He is both happy and sad—happy because he is finally describing his real feelings to Roxane and making her happy; sad because she does not know that it is he who is speaking, and because he is furthering the cause of his rival.

3. He pretends that he has fallen from outer space and describes the fanciful worlds he encountered there. He is clever and imaginative, and he is able to satirize keenly his own society.

4. She detests him but is able to toy with him to achieve her goal of keeping Christian out of danger. The audience knows Roxane's true feelings because

Rostand has let them hear her express her love for Christian.

5. The heroic ideal is a person who knows he must endure without too much complaint. Cyrano shows that he is noble and wise at the same time his heart is breaking.

Apply Background

Students may mention the section about Cyrano's many gifts as well as his underlying vulnerability and sense of inferiority as being of particular relevance to this act.

Literary Element: Imagery

1. Students may mention Cyrano's fanciful discussion of his space voyage, which contains the following imagery: *"Dust of the moon, / Asteroid fragments clinging like sleep to my eyes, / Planet-fur on my spurs, blond comet-hairs / On my coat."*

2. Almost against his will, de Guiche becomes interested in what Cyrano is telling him. Cyrano has not only a way with description but a keen eye for the right details to use with de Guiche. Students may say that this tells them Cyrano is a shrewd judge of what motivates others.

Reading Strategy: Make and Verify Predictions About Plot

1. One example is when de Guiche threatens to get rid of Cyrano by sending him off to war. Although Roxane tricks him into changing his mind at first, by the end of the act, de Guiche has found out about her scheme and, out of revenge, he sends Cyrano and Christian's regiment off to battle.

2. Students may or may not believe Cyrano will succeed. Because they already know that the play is in part a tragedy, they may predict that Cyrano will fail to win her in the end. But because Roxane and Cyrano have been revealed to be perfectly suited to each other, some students may assume that Cyrano will triumph and there will be a happy ending.

Vocabulary Practice

1. opposite
2. opposite
3. opposite
4. same
5. same

Academic Vocabulary

Not allowing Roxane and Christian to kiss was one thing Cyrano did that seemed to deviate from his purpose.

Writing

Paraphrase a Speech

Students' paraphrases should reveal their understanding of both the sentiments and overall context of Cyrano's speech.

Speaking and Listening

Performance

Students' presentations should illustrate their understanding of the selected scene. They should also incorporate:

• movement and body language
• strong attempts at characterization
• eye contact and facial expressions
• strong pacing

ACT 4

BEFORE YOU READ

Summarize

The French Roman Catholic cardinal Armand-Jean de Richelieu, an adviser to Louis XIII, led France into the Thirty Years' War, after which France became the most powerful nation in Europe.

ACTIVE READING

The simile compares musical notes to smiles. Implication: One need not have food as long as there are art and beauty.
The simile compares homeland soil to wholesome red meat and the green plains to a storm of emeralds. Implication: The memory of the homeland is as good and healthful for a soldier as food.
The simile compares the weight of Roxane's self-professed guilt to being crushed by a boulder. Implication: The torture of guilt is worse than physical pain.

INTERACTIVE READING

Literary Element: Simile

In lines 102–120, the music of the flute player is compared to the rich and pleasant life that the cadets led in Gascony.

Literary Element: Simile

He wants to take their minds off their hunger and get them thinking pleasant thoughts about home and peacetime. The arrival of de Guiche kills the mood and makes the men depressed once again.

Reading Strategy: Apply Background Knowledge

The introduction states that Cyrano's sense of inferiority shapes fills his life and his personality. His response to Roxane's proclamation that she could love a soul like Christian's even if the body and face were ugly is momentarily thrilling to Cyrano, but when Christian is killed, so are Cyrano's joy and confidence.

Reading Strategy: Apply Background Knowledge

Rostand modeled Cyrano on a real-life figure named Cyrano, a poet-soldier who actually took part in the battle at Arras. But other reasons for setting the scene there may have had more to do with the potentially tragic stakes of war.

ON-PAGE NOTE-TAKING

BIG Idea: The Tragic Vision

Students should note that Cyrano feels he must now give up all chance of love and happiness—he has failed to keep his promise to protect Christian and is perhaps about to be killed himself in a terrible battle. Because of the circumstances, his noble nature, and his feelings of inferiority, he is unable to proclaim his love to Roxane and instead offers himself up to death.

AFTER YOU READ

Respond and Think Critically

1. It identifies the commander and makes him an easier target. De Guiche drops it to avoid being shot. Cyrano identifies the scarf with a man's panache and retrieves it at great personal risk.

2. Roxane is a beautiful young woman of the educated class. She appears to be intelligent and kind but is sometimes superficial. She seems to be weary of the advances of brutish men, and she desires a lover who is both eloquent and inspiring. In the end, her love for Christian is based solely on what Cyrano's words have portrayed. Some students may say that Roxane is worthy of both their loves, maybe even a combination of the two, because she sticks to her ideals. Others may feel that Roxane is not realistic and is too concerned with pleasing herself.

3. He urges Cyrano to tell Roxane that the letters came from him. Christian is tired of living a lie.

4. Students may say that, true to her convictions, she would love Cyrano in spite of his ugliness, while others may claim she would still prefer Christian because of her inability to overcome Cyrano's physical characteristics.

5. He never takes the chance of proclaiming his love for Roxane even though he is passionately devoted to her. He is deeply afraid of being rejected. His fears about his appearance hold him back from attaining happiness.

Apply Background

Answers will vary. Students may recall Rostand's humility and apologetic behavior when he assumed his play would be a failure; they may recognize that there was a bit of Cyrano's fearful and tragic side in the author.

Literary Element: Simile

1. The similes remind the cadets of their homeland in Gascony, which lulls them into momentary happiness.
2. She feels she has underestimated Christian by focusing on his physical beauty rather than his beautiful soul. Without realizing it, she is telling Christian that she could love Cyrano, for it is Cyrano's soul she is responding to. This makes Christian see that Roxane is not truly in love with him but with Cyrano, and he therefore urges Cyrano to confess everything.

Reading Strategy: Apply Background Knowledge

1. Answers will vary. Students may mention his daring daily adventures to post his letters to Roxane or his ability to calm the starving cadets with his poetry.
2. Roxane falls in love with Cyrano's soul (though unwittingly), Christian is willing to give up Roxane when he realizes it is Cyrano she really loves, and Cyrano selflessly gives up Roxane when Christian dies. These are all romantic ideals.

Vocabulary Practice

1. same
2. same
3. opposite
4. same
5. opposite

Academic Vocabulary

It means "to offer" or "to present." Both words are verbs, but their connotations and denotations are different.

Write with Style

Apply Figurative Language (Epic Simile)

Evaluate students' essays on the strength and interest value of their comparisons and the overall cohesion and presentation of ideas.

Speaking and Listening

Literature Groups

Evaluate student discussions based on participation, use of examples from the text, interpretive skill, and collaboration.

ACT 5

BEFORE YOU READ
Write the Caption

Actors from around the world have made their mark on the legendary role of Cyrano de Bergerac.

ACTIVE READING

Situational Irony: DE GUICHE. I think I envy him, yes, Envy him—is situational irony because de Guiche has despised and worked against Cyrano earlier in the play.

Dramatic Irony: ROXANE. My future lies among the faithful—is dramatic irony because the audience knows what she does not, that she has always lived among the faithful because of Cyrano's devotion to her.

CYRANO. It's just possible, I'm afraid, I may have to go before it's dark—is dramatic irony because the audience knows what Roxane does not, that Cyrano is actually dying.

Structural Irony: ROXANE. You must live. I love you—is structural irony because it is a contradiction of her behavior throughout the play, and it comes at a point when it is too late.

INTERACTIVE READING

Literary Element: Irony

The audience knows that Cyrano has been mortally injured, but Roxane does not. He plays along with her and for quite a while she is able to sustain her belief that things are going as usual.

Literary Element: Irony

Verbal irony. Cyrano is dying; he feels he might die before it gets dark. The irony is that when he talks about leaving, Roxane assumes he is talking about going home when he is actually referring to his death.

Reading Strategy: Synthesize

Cyrano in essence counts out his positive traits and his negative ones. He finds himself lacking in many areas but gives himself credit in others. In the end, he leaves this world with his *panache* intact. Audiences might take this a number of ways, but the overall message seems to be that one should take hold of both life and love in order to live to the fullest.

Reading Strategy: Synthesize

It is comedic because Cyrano, a swashbuckler to the end, is battling death, but he needs help from a nearby tree to remain upright. In the larger sense it is tragic because Cyrano is dying and leaving Roxane behind in the very moment she has realized she loves him.

ON-PAGE NOTE-TAKING

BIG Idea: The Tragic Vision

Students may say that in a sense Cyrano overcomes his tragic flaw in death, becoming as beautiful to Roxane as Christian ever was. Though he loves her, he also says she is his friend, and as her friend he at last is able to be honest with her about his true feelings.

AFTER YOU READ

Respond and Think Critically

1. Cyrano visits Roxane weekly, is very poor but allows no one to help him, is still witty, and makes enemies by attacking injustice and other evils in his writings. Fifteen years have passed, and Rostand needs to tell readers and viewers what has happened since the battle.

2. De Guiche has grudgingly come to respect Cyrano because of his integrity.

3. Cyrano knows the letter by heart and can recite it with his eyes closed. Students may say Roxane was surprised because her self-centeredness and inability to read clues would have blinded her to the truth. Others may argue that the clues were so obvious that she must have at least suspected the truth.

4. It is autumn, the time of year when things in nature are dying gloriously. Roxane calls the season the "gentle end," de Guiche speaks of the "dry rustle of dead illusions," and Cyrano refers to the leaves falling with panache and grace, and the death of the year echoes Christian's death long ago as well, foreshadowing Cyrano's impending death.

5. Students may say that the idea of love that lasts a lifetime, even if unspoken, inspires hope. They may also mention that Cyrano's *panache,* which he takes with him into death, is a hopeful human attribute.

Apply Background

Students may say that in this final act, the play's language, wit, emotion, and themes helped them appreciate the lure of the role of Cyrano for actors around the globe.

Literary Element: Irony

1. It is ironic in that the playwright is poking fun at Moliere, because Rostand's play uses the time period, the level of language, and many of the theatrical devices of Moliere.

2. This is an example of verbal irony because he says he says again and again that he does not love Roxane when it is clear that he means exactly the opposite.

Reading Strategy: Synthesize

1. Students may compare the play to specific works by the Greek tragedians or Shakespeare. They may mention that the themes of love and self-sacrifice, as well as commonly held perceptions about physical beauty being the ultimate attribute are universal and are found in a great many contemporary films and plays, although specific examples will vary.

2. Some students may believe that Cyrano kept silent only because he feared rejection about his appearance. Others may feel that Cyrano's motives were more noble and that it was respect for Christian's memory that held him back.

Vocabulary Practice

1. The sentence structure implies that clowns are sometimes taken to be mere fools when in fact they are often highly trained professionals.

2. The phrase "thick with garbage, oil, and chemical runoff" explains why the river is defiled, or polluted.

3. Giving in quickly is a behavior that contrasts with *obstinate,* which means "stubborn."

4. The word *calm* is a synonym for *stoic.*

5. Rat are examples of vermin.

Academic Vocabulary

The phrase "delirious and near death" describes a person who is not in his right mind. *Coherent* means lucid or rational.

Write with Style

Apply Irony

Students' eulogies should be evaluated for use of verbal, dramatic, and structural irony and an understanding of the complexity of Cyrano's character.

Speaking and Listening

Oral Report

Students' oral reports should be evaluated on

- completeness of information
- coherence
- understanding of the two versions
- public-speaking techniques

NOVEL AFTER YOU READ

WORK WITH RELATED READINGS

The Masterpieces

Amoia defines Cyrano's panache as his desire to be "admirable in all," his love of sincerity and courage, and his disdain for convention. Students' answers should be supported with examples from the text.

"Cyrano de Bergerac"/"Cyrano" in English

Students may cite Cyrano's timeless character or the simple fact that the play is entertaining, regardless of its implausibility and exaggerated ideals.

Beauty: When the Other Dancer Is the Self

Walker can finally see herself as beautiful, while Cyrano never sees himself as beautiful. However, both Walker and Cyrano have self-respect.

On Falling in Love

He would probably agree with Stevenson. Christian ultimately gives up on his relationship with Roxane because he realizes he is loved for a quality that is not really his.

Strangers in Love

The knowledge that Christian might die serves to heighten Roxane's sense of what is important in her relationship with Christian/Cyrano, leading her to a higher level of admiration for the man she thinks she has fallen in love with.

CONNECT TO OTHER LITERATURE

Hero Answers will vary. Both characters have many gifts, each makes a name for himself and rises to prominence in society. Both are intelligent, but Cyrano is also very witty. Both have wisdom and strength, but despite this, each is brought down by a tragic flaw. For Oedipus the flaw is his pride, which leads him to reckless behavior. For Cyrano it is his inability to see past his physical appearance.

Imagery Unlike the chorus's assessment of Oedipus's plight, the imagery Cyrano uses to greet his own death is full of the same vigor and panache he has displayed throughout the play. Instead of giving in to a "black sea of terror" (failure and death), Cyrano mentions bright stars, white plumes, and a diamond in the ash. In other words, Oedipus goes out a broken man while Cyrano is elevated to new heights.

Irony In the excerpt, Oedipus, a once-powerful king, has been reduced to powerlessness. He makes demands, but is no longer "master of all things." This contrasts with the irony of Cyrano's feeling powerless due to his appearance when he has so many heroic traits.

Write About It

Answers will vary.

RESPOND THROUGH WRITING

Expository Essay

Evaluate students' essays on

- variety of sources
- completeness of chart
- strong point of view
- coherence

Nectar in a Sieve

Kamala Markandaya

Nectar in a Sieve *by Kamala Markandaya*

Nectar in a Sieve, the first published novel of Indian-born author Kamala Markandaya, provides a moving and believable portrait of life in a remote Indian agricultural village during the mid-twentieth century. Although the story is filled with tragedy—the Hindu family at the center of the novel suffers the deprivations of extreme poverty and is forced to adapt to the gradual modernization of Indian society—the characters find strength in their love for one another. In 1955, a year after *Nectar in a Sieve* was first published, the American Library Association named it a notable book. Today, it is considered to be a classic of modern Indian literature and is a perennial entry on world literature "must read" lists.

Teachers should note that the novel depicts the subordinate status of women in a culture bound by tradition and includes veiled descriptions of a young woman's descent into prostitution. Before assigning students to read the novel, review it carefully to determine whether it is appropriate for your students.

Synopsis

Rukmani, an Indian peasant woman, looks back over her life. After her parents arrange her marriage to a farmer named Nathan, she leaves her home to live in her husband's hut in a village in southern India. She eventually bears seven children. The family's life depends on the quality of the harvests. The oldest child, Ira, is married, but her husband returns her to her parents because she is unable to become pregnant. Village life is ominously disrupted when a tannery is built. The family's economic status improves when the two oldest sons, Arjun and Thambi, get work in the tannery. They are forced to leave the tannery after they lead a strike.

A drought ruins the rice crop, and starvation claims the life of Rukmani's youngest son, Kuti. Raja is killed by tannery guards who accuse him of stealing. A conflict with Kunthi, a promiscuous neighbor, results in Kunthi's blackmailing Rukmani and Nathan and demanding food for her silence. To bring in money, Ira becomes a prostitute. Her occupation is revealed one night when Rukmani attacks her, believing her to be Kunthi. Selvam becomes a British doctor's assistant at the new hospital the doctor is building. Ira gives birth to an albino baby boy; his father is unknown.

The family learns that their rented land is to be sold for an expansion of the tannery. Rukmani and Nathan decide to go to live with Murugan in a distant city. Rukmani and Nathan learn that Murugan has disappeared. They seek shelter in a Hindu temple, where their money and few remaining possessions are stolen. Destitute, they find work in a stone quarry. Their protecting angel is a young, streetwise beggar named Puli, who suffers from leprosy. One day while toiling in the quarry, Nathan collapses. He dies, and Rukmani returns to the village with Puli, whom she and Nathan had adopted.

Portrait of India

Have students draw on their prior knowledge of India.

- Draw a word web on the board, with the word *India* in the center.

- Ask students to help you complete the web with information about India.

- Have students explain how they learned the cultural, social, or historical information that they offer.

- Conclude the activity by explaining that *Nectar in a Sieve* is widely admired for its portrait of Indian village life. Challenge students to be aware of how the novel reinforces or conflicts with the information they provided during this activity.

Acceptance

Help students explore the novel's philosophy of acceptance.

- Write the following sentence on the board, identifying it as one that appears in the novel: "Bend like the grass, that you do not break."

- Ask students to rephrase the statement in their own words.

- Have students respond to the statement. Do they agree with it? Is it sound advice on how to live? What are some possible benefits and disadvantages of following the advice? What other phrases do they know that either echo or contrast with the statement? Name some persons from life or literature who either follow or reject the advice.

- Conclude by saying that some of the characters in *Nectar in a Sieve* follow this

advice and others do not. Suggest that students look for characters' attitudes toward this philosophy of life.

Two-Way Street

Help students examine the mutual obligations of parents and children.

- On the board, create a two-column chart with these headings: What Children Owe Their Parents and What Parents Owe Their Children.

- Ask students to work in pairs to come up with five entries for each column.

- Ask each pair to read an entry; write the entry in the appropriate column.

- Discuss issues and questions raised by the students' suggestions.

- End the activity by explaining that one of the themes in *Nectar in a Sieve* is the relationship between parents and children.

Women in Society

Help students explore how custom and tradition can affect the ways in which women lead their lives.

- Ask students to help you make a list of customs and traditions that influence the ways in which women in U.S. society live.

- After a dozen entries, ask students to decide whether the customs have positive or negative effects on women and in what ways. Have students explain their responses.

- Conclude by asking students to pay attention as they read to ways in which custom and tradition influence the main character's life in an Indian village.

RELATED READINGS	MAKING CONNECTIONS TO *Nectar in a Sieve*
Pictures of Marriage by Ved Mehta (Glencoe's *Literature Library*, BLM page 25)	**In reminiscences of his childhood in a Hindu household, noted writer Ved Mehta remembers his family's preparations for a traditional marriage ceremony.** • Ask students to think about recent wedding festivities that they have heard about from any source—from actual participation to news accounts of celebrity weddings. Together, identify customs and traditions that are common to many ceremonies in this country. • After students read the selection, ask them to name some of the fears and emotions Mehta shares with Rukmani on her wedding day.
Letter to Lord Irwin *and* **About That Letter** by Mahatma Gandhi **Rice** by Chemmanam Chacko (Glencoe's *Literature Library*, BLM page 26)	**In his quest for independence for India, Mahatma Gandhi perfected the strategy of nonviolent protest. While Indians could rejoice as a nation in being free of foreign domination, independence also meant changes in their way of life, as the speaker in "Rice" tells us.** • Ask students to recall what they have learned about civil disobedience and nonviolent protests in U.S. history. Speculate with students on the effectiveness of this strategy in different times of protest, such as the American colonists' protest against British rule, women's drive for voting rights, and the Civil Rights movement. • After students read the novel, list injustices that Rukmani's fellow citizens might protest with nonviolent demonstrations. • Point out that the press—newspapers, radio, and television—can be used by others to promote special causes and to spread information favorable to themselves. Ask students to name some groups that use the press for purposes other than news.
Snatched from Death translated by Dwijendra Nath Neog **In India, Marriages** **Made by Computer** by Sheila Tefft (Glencoe's *Literature Library*, BLM page 27)	**Folklore tells us about the long history of traditions that are still practiced today. Newspaper accounts often tell us how traditions are being overturned.** • Ask students to think about some marriage customs that are based on traditions in their cultures. Then discuss how these traditions may be changing. • Lead a discussion on the ways in which the computer has changed many facets of our lives.
Work Without Hope by Samuel Taylor Coleridge (Glencoe's *Literature Library*, BLM page 28)	**Markandaya took the title of her novel from this Coleridge poem.** • Before students read the poem, define *allusion*. • After students read, ask them to brainstorm connections between the poem and the novel.
from A Passage **to India** by Santha Rama Rau (Glencoe's *Literature Library*, BLM page 29)	**This play is based on a novel that has become known as one of the classic examinations of the differences between East and West.** • Ask students to think about some of the areas in which misunderstandings might have arisen between the British rulers and the early American colonists. Would the colonists have had an interest in court etiquette, royal protocol, or other matters that concerned people in London? • As students read *Nectar in a Sieve*, alert them to look for examples of differences between the cultures of Kennington and Rukmani. • After students read this selection, have them compare Fielding and Kennington. How are the two Englishmen alike in their feelings about India?

All answers are sample answers except those for Vocabulary Practice.

CHAPTERS 1–13

BEFORE YOU READ
Write the Caption

India's city streets flood during a monsoon.

ACTIVE READING

Answers will vary. Students may say: *sight,* "a rocket would tear into the sky, break and pour out its riches like precious jewels"; *taste,* "holding a stick of sugar cane nearly as tall as himself"; *smell,* "the smell of oil was everywhere, heavy and pungent";. *hearing,* "the drumbeats died to a murmur"; *touch,* "I pushed my way through the crush."

INTERACTIVE READING
Literary Element: Point of View

The narration reveals her inner thoughts, her deep love for her children and her husband, and her worries for their well-being. She thinks of others before herself and is willing to give up her own rations in order to provide the very best she can for her family.

Literary Element: Point of View

She fears that they do not have a large enough dowry to win Ira a good husband. She is pained that her daughter must leave her, and she knows the loneliness and fear a young wife feels at first—Rukmani has felt it herself. She has saved "rice and dhal and ghee, jars of oil" and more for months in order to have a feast for her daughter's wedding.

Reading Strategy: Interpret Imagery

Images such as the uprooted trees, ripped off roofs, and corrugated iron thrown up into trees or into the walls of still standing structures creates a scene of utter destruction, as well as feelings of shock and amazement at the terrific and terrible force of the storm. The senses of sight and feeling (of texture) dominate.

Reading Strategy: Interpret Imagery

Students may say they hear the drums and share the narrator's sense of doom. They may also say they see the cleared streets and signs of rebuilding, which enables them to share a sense of hopefulness with the narrator. Students may also say they feel the precious cache of rice tucked into the narrator's sari and share in the secure feeling that it gives her.

ON-PAGE NOTE-TAKING
BIG Idea: A Place in Society

As a woman, Rukmani's fate is determined in part by her father's position, her place in the birth order, and her female gender. Place in the birth order affects how much dowry she can receive; her father's status affects whom she can marry. These factors, in turn, affect how financially well off she might be in the future through the type of marriage she might make. Because her father lacks status and she lacks a dowry, she ends up married to a poor tenant farmer and condemned to life in an unfinished mud hut.

AFTER YOU READ
Respond and Think Critically

1. Rukmani sees a garland of mango leaves, a symbol of happiness and good fortune. The leaves have become dry and rattle in the wind. The garland may be a symbolic hint that their good fortune will dry up.

2. It has brought more people to the village and Rukmani can make a profit by selling to them. There is now an opportunity for jobs other than rice farming. On the negative side, it brings pollution, noise, and obstructed views of the natural surroundings Rukmani so enjoyed. Her sons argue for more money from their employers, which only results in them losing their jobs and being right back where they started. Markandaya shows that the coming of industry brings more complexity to the villagers' lives, but overall, it doesn't really seem to change them for the better or the worse.

3. Rukmani objects and fears that the tannery will destroy their way of life; the other women see potential benefits. Students' answers will vary but should be supported with sound reasons.

4. They go to work in Ceylon because they have been fired from the tannery. They realize that a modern economy requires that workers go to where the work is, that employers hold all the cards, and that the company's self-interest will ensure that it keeps its promises to workers. Rukmani believes that it would be better for them to stay at home and keep the family together despite the lack of work.

5. Rukmani is disappointed because male heirs contribute to the family, while dowries for female heirs drain family resources. Women play a less-valued role in the culture.

Apply Background

Answers will vary. Students may suggest that knowing Markandaya's background will help them to understand her ideas about rural life in India and therefore give them a better understanding of the themes of the novel.

Literary Element: Point of View

1. Students may say they feel very close to the story because they can hear Rukmani's voice, which is full of details, and because her tone, her word choices, her images, and her sentences all have a powerful effect on their emotions as well as on what they learn. Some students may say that despite the first-person narration, the story is too remote from their own time and place to allow them to feel close to the narrator or to her experience.

2. Kenny is often frustrated at how Rukmani and Nathan live out their destiny without trying to fight it. If the story were told from Kenny's perspective, the reader may be more likely to feel that Rukmani and Nathan are foolish and ignorant of the ways in which they could improve their condition. If Kenny were the narrator, the reader would be less likely to understand Rukmani's great love for her husband and children and the depth of her internal struggle. The reader would, however, probably have a better understanding of all Kenny has sacrificed in order to try to help the rural Indian people.

Reading Strategy: Interpret Imagery

1. Answers will vary widely. Students may suggest imagery related to the large and abundant vegetables, including pumpkins, that Rukmani grows or images of the food, setting, and celebrating for Ira's wedding.

2. When the paddy is green and beautiful, and when it is filled abundantly with water, as well as wildlife such as fish and birds, life is good for the family, and all is well. But when the river is dry and the shoots in the paddy are tipped with brown and then stained as if with "disease," life is choked out, and hope is lost.

Vocabulary Practice

injunctions: definition – limitations imposed on a person's freedom, etymology – Latin *injunctionem* means "command." Sample sentences will vary.

ravenous: definition – extremely hungry, etymology – Old French *ravinos* means "rapacious, violent." Sample sentences will vary.

reproach: definition – to blame or criticize, etymology – Old French *reproache* means "to blame, bring up against." Sample sentences will vary.

solace: definition – any form of comfort, etymology – Latin *solacium* means "to console, sooth." Sample sentences will vary.

taciturn: definition – silent, reluctant to talk, etymology – Latin *tacitus* means "silent." Sample sentences will vary.

Academic Vocabulary

consult

Definition: to ask guidance from

Synonyms: ask, see, check

Antonyms: avoid, ignore, reject

Sentence or image will vary.

Write With Style

Apply Imagery

Students' essays should

- create a single dominant emotional impression of a place

- include a variety of appropriate imagery, especially imagery based on senses other than sight

- organize ideas in a spatial order that is appropriate to the topic

Connect to Content Areas

Social Studies

Students' written reports should

- compare the culture and customs of industrialized and traditional India

- compare the culture and customs of rural and urban India

- use relevant details and specific examples, including correctly formatted citations from various sources

- be clearly focused and well organized

- include a correctly formatted bibliography of sources

CHAPTERS 14–23

BEFORE YOU READ

Summarize

Followers of Hinduism, one of the world's major religions, worship many gods and believe in the importance of karma, the moral law of cause and effect, as well as reincarnation.

ACTIVE READING

Effects: portions of rice are meted out carefully; Kunthi comes to get rice from Rukmani; the family experiences the sensations of grave hunger; Kuti becomes seriously ill; Kunthi receives the rice from Nathan; the family must forage to eat, including on grass which causes them to become ill.

Causes: The tannery owners want the land; Nathan and Rukmani do not own the land; Nathan and Rukmani have no reserve cash; Nathan and Rukmani have no one to help them.

INTERACTIVE READING
Literary Element: Diction

Rukmani sounds formal because she describes herself as "laden" and "well pleased" and because she uses sophisticated phrases and sophisticated words such as "confounding" and "contemptuously." She also spontaneously creates figurative language in her speech ("a whore's tale. . . . "). Biswas, on the other hand, uses no sophisticated language and relies on short, to-the-point sentences and fragments.

Literary Element: Diction

Kali's diction is least sophisticated: she uses everyday words arranged in everyday phrases and sentences, as well as the colloquial sounding "Who ever heard . . . ?" her speech makes her sound uneducated and crude. Of the characters, Selvam sounds most sophisticated and formal, such as in the formal sounding "Who is to say . . . and "I should have thought. . . . ". His speech reflects dignity and thoughtfulness. The narrator is also formal in her use of words and phrases such as *equably, affronted, perished, lightened of suspense,* and *rebuking.*

Reading Strategy: Analyze Cause and Effect

Nathan suggests that "when the time comes" they will have the strength to farm, as if fate will play a part in the process of their recovery. Rukmani suggests that the gods might intervene by ripening the fields in less than three weeks.

Reading Strategy: Analyze Cause and Effect

Many answers are possible. Students may go all the way back to Ira's position as a woman in her society and the fact that her husband "returned" her, like a piece of faulty merchandise, for her supposed failure to bear children. Students should cite Kuti's illness, and may cite hunger; poverty; the previous failures of the rice crop or overall dependence on the land, especially in a tenant farmer situation; as well as other causes.

ON-PAGE NOTE-TAKING
BIG Idea: A Place in Society

The passage shows that there is no justice for them or opportunity for justice. A person can be killed for an act of thievery, or an act of supposed thievery. Rukmani and her family have no recourse—and no true sense that they ought to have recourse.

AFTER YOU READ
Respond and Think Critically

1. Nathan reveals that he is the father of Kunthi's sons. Rukmani reveals that she visited Dr. Kennington for medical help. Students' answers may vary, but students should note that the confessions bring the characters closer together.

2. Ira's sacrifice of herself for Kuti helps show the theme of individual struggle; it also helps to show the futility of the struggle against forces greater than individuals, because Kuti dies anyway.

3. Using the present tense can make an episode seem more immediate and real, as if it were happening before the reader's eyes rather than in the past. Markandaya may have wanted to stress the painfulness of this moment.

4. Kennington believes people should cry out against injustice, make their needs known, and battle for what is right. Rukmani believes a person should be strong and accept suffering and deprivation in life, an attitude which she believes will cleanse the soul. Students' answers will vary but should be supported with reasonable arguments.

5. The tannery changes the town and the ways of life, but it does not help Nathan and Rukmani in any way. In fact, it diminishes them greatly. One son dies at the tannery. Two others leave forever as a result of events at the tannery. Nathan and Rukmani themselves become exiles from their own land and way of life because of the tannery.

Apply Background

Answers will vary. Students may say that the end of British rule in India did nothing to help the rural poor.

Literary Element: Diction

1. Both speakers are educated and formal. Kenny, however, is a little more to the point and abrupt, whereas Rukmani sounds more sophisticated with her longer, more complicated sentences that often display poetic word choices as well as elevated language.

2. Students may say that formal diction helps Rukmani to appear part of the fray of life and yet above it all somehow, because she can express her observations with such sophistication and grace. Apt word choices help the reader enter her world and examine her character.

Reading Strategy: Analyze Cause and Effect

1. Kenny keeps returning to the village because he feels he has a mission there. Also, over time, he appears to have nowhere else to go: his marriage ends.

2. Kenny's presence gives Selvam the chance to leave agricultural work without having to turn to the tannery. Instead, he can work with Kenny doing work that is meaningful and from which he might learn a great deal. Kenny's presence gives Selvam a chance for dignity in his work life.

Vocabulary Practice

1. f, 2. c, 3. e, 4. g, 5. b

Academic Vocabulary

Sustain means to "keep or to keep going." The phrases "even after" and "still able" hint at the definition.

Write With Style
Apply Diction

Students' essays should

- create a dialogue set in a specific place
- create two characters, one of whom both narrates in the first person and takes part in the dialogue
- convey information about characters through their diction, especially through a contrast in formal and informal diction
- use chronological order and correct paragraphs

Speaking and Listening
Oral Interpretation

Students' performances should

- reflect an understanding of the idea alluded to in the book's title, through choice of scene and explanation of scene
- include well-chosen and thoughtful dramatic additions (sound effects, emphasis of words or lines, pauses, etc) that reflect a good understanding of the scene
- be performed with appropriate volume, pacing, enunciation, and eye contact
- include an explanation of the dramatic choices made, and how they helped to reflect the idea alluded to in the book's title

CHAPTERS 24–30

BEFORE YOU READ
Write the Caption

Mother Teresa comforts an Indian orphan.

ACTIVE READING

Sentence: "You brood too much and think only of the trials, not of the joys that are still with us."; Balanced Elements: nouns—trials, joys; Effect: emphasizes the optimism of the character Nathan, who speaks these words; creates irony for the reader who sees the trials and almost no joy

Sentence: "I noticed one or two glances exchanged, pitying yet scornful, which said as plainly as words, These are simple careless country folk."; Balanced Elements: adjectives—pitying, scornful; Effect: shows that those who judge Rukmani and Nathan know their plight very well and yet still judge them and stand apart from them, emphasizing their aloneness and their pitiable condition

Sentence: "There was a taste of salt and of the fresh sweetness of rainwater."; Balanced Elements: nouns—salt and sweetness; Effect: increases drama of scene and sympathy for narrator, who has been crying in the rain

INTERACTIVE READING
Literary Element: Antithesis

Several answers are possible: "Free meals were given only in the evening, not in the morning." The opposites are the nouns *morning* and *evening*. The sentence helps to emphasize the characters' plight and their hunger; "I shook off the gathered people, who parted to let me through, then closed their ranks as I knelt beside them." The opposites are the verbs *parted* and *closed*. These verbs emphasize the drama of the scene and make it more visual.

Literary Element: Antithesis

The use of one antithetical pairing after another has a graceful, rhythmic effect. Ironically, this effect emphasizes the piling up of misfortunes for Nathan and Rukmani.

Reading Strategy: Connect to Contemporary Issues

Answers will vary. Children in poverty are much more likely to suffer abuse and disease. They learn at a young age their need to protect themselves and survive in a very harsh world. Many are witness to violent crime and abuse and have to learn to live with the emotional scars of such pain.

Reading Strategy: Connect to Contemporary Issues

Answers will vary. Even amidst their hardship, children who grow up poor in America are still children just the same—like the Indian children who Rukmani describes as "forgetful of their pains" and playing in the sun. But at the same time, kids living in poverty in the U.S. are more prone to turn to gangs or drugs in order to try and survive their difficult position in life. The Indian kids fight voraciously for survival, with "teeth bared, nails clawing, ready, predatory like animals" when food falls off a nearby cart.

ON-PAGE NOTE-TAKING

BIG Idea: A Place in Society

Murugan is a servant and rootless. His home is where the best wages are paid. Rukmani and Nathan are at the mercy of anyone who is richer or of a higher status. They must wait even to ask about their son until the doctor comes around to the subject; they are at the doctor's mercy for kindness and sustenance.

AFTER YOU READ

Respond and Think Critically

1. Metaphorical connections include that the journey to the town is toward an unknown goal; Nathan and Rukmani have no choice but to take the journey; they have few possessions; the journey is long and difficult; like the peasants, the bullock accepts his torment; they are victimized along the way; they are small drops in an ocean of poor people.

2. She reads and writes for illiterate people. Her literacy has been considered a foolish skill for a peasant woman, but now it enables Rukmani to earn some money.

3. Leaving out specific details makes the story more universal, the story of India rather than the tale of a few particular Indians.

4. Rukmani worries that Nathan will be angry, and she feels she has foolishly spent their money on nonessentials. Students' answers may vary but some may say that buying small extras can mean very much to people in her situation because it makes them feel they have some freedom and discretion, rewards them for their backbreaking work, and lets them do something nice for other people.

5. Some students may say that the ending is consistent with the beginning: the characters have nothing and little hope of having anything, yet they do have each other and an attitude that is accepting of their place in the world. Other students may say that by the end the characters, and Rukmani in particular, have descended to an even lower place, for Rukmani is old, she has lost Nathan and almost all her children in various ways, and those left to her include a child without fingers and an outcast albino.

Apply Background

Answers will vary. Students may say that understanding the work of Mother Teresa, and therefore the great need of the poor in India, will help the reader to relate to the images of the poor and suffering in the novel.

Literary Element: Antithesis

1. Students may say that antithesis helps show the contrast between what is and what ought to be: for example, the characters would wish for pity, not scorn; capital, not charity; sweetness, not salt. They might also say it helps to increase the drama of scenes or that, in some cases, it creates irony.

2. Answers will vary widely. Sample: "Leave behind your silence and turn it into screams of outrage."

Reading Strategy: Connect to Contemporary Issues

1. Answers will vary. A person today would probably struggle to find work, money, and food just as Rukmani and Nathan did. Although help could come through homeless shelters and charities, life would be just as brutal and dangerous on the streets today as it was for Rukmani and Nathan then.

2. Some students may say that Markandaya would view globalization with the same eyes: as something that leaves the poor behind or worsens their condition. Others may say that globalization brings more opportunities than industrialization brings and may eventually increase chances for education and better medical care; therefore, Markandaya might have viewed it differently.

Vocabulary Practice

1. predatory, 2. poignancy, 3. none, 4. wily,
5. inexorably, 6. none, 7. amity

Academic Vocabulary

Answers will vary.

Writing

Write a Letter to the Editor

Students' letters should

- be addressed to the editor of a newspaper
- focus on poverty at the local, state, national, or international level
- incorporate at least one example of antithesis and use it effectively to further the argument

Connect to Content Areas

Art

Students' art projects should

- portray at least one famous characteristic of the god or goddess

- be completed in a medium that helps to show this characteristic
- reflect research and understanding of the god or goddess
- include an oral report with appropriate tone of voice, body language, and eye contact that thoroughly explains and supports artistic choices made

NOVEL AFTER YOU READ

WORK WITH RELATED READINGS
Pictures of Marriage

Rukmani's family did not expect to find a rich bridegroom for her because they were poor and she was not beautiful. Even though Rukmani and Nathan had little for a dowry, they found a bridegroom from a well-to-do family because their daughter was attractive. Cousin Sheila's engagement was called off because the bridegroom was overweight. Marriage was not even considered for Cousin Vidya because she had misshapen hands. Mamaji believes that her son Mehta has no chance of marrying because he is blind.

Letter to Lord Irwin *and* About That Letter; Rice

Students may say that the first letter relates most clearly because it addresses the specific issue of land revenue, the few rich zamindars, the ryots (peasants), and the need to change this system. They may also say that "Rice" relates most clearly because it creates a poignant picture of the life that Nathan and Rukmani lived, especially Nathan, and shows how industrialization brings overwhelming change.

Snatched from Death; In India, Marriages Made by Computer

"Snatched from Death" echoes the tremendous dependence that a married woman has on her husband, as shown in *Nectar in a Sieve*: "I have no home but where he is." The newspaper article shows that marriages are still arranged, as they are in the novel, but that the go-between is often no longer a family member or respected member of the community, such as Old Granny, but a computerized matchmaking service.

Work Without Hope

Coleridge's poem contrasts nature's ongoing work with man's need for hope if he is to continue his work. Markandaya's characters can continue to work because they continue to hope.

A Passage to India

Answers will vary. Students may say that the two men are sensitive to other people's feelings because the men see other people as individual human beings and not stereotypes.

CONNECT TO OTHER LITERATURE

Point of View: The point of view in the parable is third person. Jesus (the narrator) is not telling his own story; he is telling the story of a father and a son.

Diction: As in *Nectar in a Sieve*, the diction is formal. In contrast to *Nectar in a Sieve*, the diction of all the characters is no less formal than the diction of the narrator is.

Antithesis: Students may say that the repeated opposites *dead* and *alive, lost* and *found* are even more dramatic and obvious in this parable, and help to form the very lesson of the parable, than the antitheses are in *Nectar in a Sieve*. They may also note that the examples in the parable do not express irony.

Talk About It

Students may say that the father who rejoices at the return of his son shows acceptance of what happens to him in life, just as Rukmani accepts her fate and embraces all that happens to her, including the changed status of her daughter and her albino grandchild. On the other hand, students may say that such a parable and philosophy are alien to Rukmani, who cannot choose to act in a generous way or in any other way, but who is, instead, always acted upon by forces greater than herself.

RESPOND THROUGH WRITING
Autobiographical Narrative

Students' autobiographical narratives should

- use first-person point of view
- be set in a place where they live now or used to live
- use traditional story structure to convey the experience
- reflect on the significance of the experience, including causes and effects that may range from fate and karma to societal, cultural, or familial factors

Picture Bride

Yoshiko Uchida

Picture Bride *by Yoshiko Uchida*

Picture Bride is a novel inspired by the hundreds of Japanese women who immigrated to the United States in the early nineteen hundreds to enter into arranged marriages. The novel chronicles the life of one Japanese picture bride from 1917 through the early years of World War II. Like many of Uchida's other writings, *Picture Bride* reveals the struggles that Japanese Americans faced during this period, when strong anti-Asian sentiments were widespread in the United States.

Synopsis

In 1917 Hana Omiya leaves what she sees as a limited life in Japan to sail to the United States to become the wife of a Japanese shopkeeper, Taro Takeda, whom she has never met. After arriving in Oakland, California, Hana is disappointed with Taro and his struggling business and has difficulty adapting to American customs. She is, however, quickly welcomed into Taro's close community of friends.

One of those friends is Kiyoshi Yamaka, a handsome young man who shares the aching loneliness of other single men in his community. Yamaka is attracted to Hana's youth, beauty, and high spirits, and Hana returns his affection. Soon it is obvious to nearly everyone—including Hana's husband—that the two are in love. Hana breaks off the relationship but has lost Taro's trust and respect. She deeply regrets having hurt and humiliated her husband and resolves to be a good and loyal wife.

Yamaka dies during the influenza epidemic of 1918. Hana, who is pregnant, also becomes ill and nearly dies. Her infant son is born prematurely after she falls down a flight of stairs. The baby dies shortly after birth. Later, Hana gives birth to a daughter, Mary, and the family moves to a small house in a white neighborhood. Hana grows in strength as she takes care of her family and a friend in need of support, learns to live with the prejudice of her white neighbors, takes a job as a maid to earn extra money, and helps save Taro's shop when he falls deeply into debt.

Taro and Hana grow closer as they work together to improve their shop and watch their daughter become a young woman. Although Hana is proud of her daughter, she is bothered that Mary seems much more American than Japanese. Hana and Mary grow apart and cannot relate well to each other. The Takedas are bitterly disappointed when Mary, rejecting her Japanese heritage and the wishes of her parents, leaves college, marries a white man, and moves away to Nevada—all without consulting her parents or even saying good-bye to them.

After the Japanese bombing of Pearl Harbor in December 1941, the Takedas and other Japanese Americans on the West Coast are forced into detention camps. While at Topaz Camp in Utah, Taro is shot and killed by a guard. When Mary and her husband visit Hana and see the terrible conditions at the camp, they try to convince Hana to get clearance to leave and move in with them. Hana, however, will not leave Taro, who is buried just outside the camp. Showing the same independence and strength of spirit that helped her through difficult times in the past, she vows to stay and someday take Taro back to Oakland, bury him next to their son, and reclaim their shop.

Survival Skills

Relate events in the novel to events in students' own lives.

- Tell students that the characters in *Picture Bride* struggle to survive difficult circumstances by searching for creative solutions and by drawing on inner strengths. You might ask students to recall times when they have had to deal with difficult circumstances. Ask them to think about specific survival skills they used. You may wish to invite volunteers to share their experiences with the class.

- Have pairs of students discuss how each of the scenarios listed below might make them feel. Then ask them to list ways in which they might try to cope with each situation.

  – You have moved to a place where you do not know anyone and must adapt to unfamiliar customs.

  – A close friend or family member moves far away.

  – You feel that you can no longer communicate with a friend or family member with whom you once had a close relationship.

  – You are made to feel different and unwelcome by people in your community.

  – You are forced to leave your home quickly and can take only a few items with you.

Cultural Diversity

Examine the place of cultural diversity in the novel and in society today.

- Invite students to identify ways in which they have experienced cultures or customs different from their own (by traveling to foreign countries, trying different foods, reading books, listening to different kinds of music, sharing holidays or customs with friends or neighbors from different cultural backgrounds).

- Tell students that cultural differences are sometimes met with fear and hostility, as they will learn when reading *Picture Bride*. Invite students to explain why some people feel threatened by the presence of those from different cultural backgrounds. What are some ways to deal with such fears and prejudices?

The Melting Pot

Discuss cultural diversity and cultural assimilation.

- Remind students that the United States has long been a nation of immigrants, populated by people from different countries and backgrounds. In 1782 J. Hector Saint John de Crèvecoeur, a French immigrant living in New York, wrote, "Here individuals of all nations are melted into a new race of men, whose labours and posterity will one day cause great changes in the world." Invite students to discuss whether they think that the United States truly consists of people from different countries who have "melted into a new race." Also ask whether they believe that de Crèvecoeur's prediction has come true. Have Americans caused "great changes in the world"?

- Ask students whether they believe that people of different cultural backgrounds should try to "melt together"? What if such melting results in a loss of cultural identity? Explain that different characters in *Picture Bride* must struggle with these issues.

RELATED READINGS	MAKING CONNECTIONS TO *Picture Bride*
Natsu Okuyama Ozawa—A Japanese Woman Remembers by June Namias (Glencoe's *Literature Library,* BLM page 25)	**The experiences of an actual Asian immigrant of the 1920s are similar to the experiences portrayed by the author of *Picture Bride*.** • Read aloud a few current news clips about immigrants and immigration policies in the United States. Have students discuss challenges that modern immigrants face. • Discuss with students how the experiences of immigrants today differ from those of Asian immigrants in the 1920s.
from **Nisei Daughter** by Monica Sone (Glencoe's *Literature Library,* BLM page 26)	**In her autobiography, Monica Sone describes her immigrant parents' early experiences in the United States and her childhood as a second-generation Japanese American.** • Have students make a list of words describing Monica as a five-year-old. • Ask students to offer explanations for Monica's reluctance to go to Japanese school. Does it have anything to do with her ancestry, or is it a child's reluctance to give up her free afternoons?
Topaz: City of Dust by Yoshiko Uchida (Glencoe's *Literature Library,* BLM page 27)	**In this nonfiction piece, Yoshiko Uchida gives a firsthand account of day-to-day life in a detention camp. She used her firsthand knowledge in *Picture Bride* to portray the experiences of her characters.** • Ask students to imagine what it would be like to choose only the bare essentials for family living and board a bus for an unknown location. Remind them that they would be assured of having a room to live in and bedding.
Sent from the Capital to Her Elder Daughter by Otomo No Sakanoe (Glencoe's *Literature Library,* BLM page 28)	**This poem, written by a mother for her child, examines the pain of separation, particularly when parents and their children must live far apart with little hope of a reunion.** • Remind students that in the novel *Picture Bride,* mothers and daughters were separated by great distances and different cultures and traditions. • Ask students to imagine living in the early nineteen hundreds and leaving their families and friends to make a new life on another continent. Have students freewrite for five to seven minutes on how they would feel.

Rain Music
 	
by Longhang Nguyen
 	
(Glencoe's *Literature Library,* BLM page 29)
	This poignant story centers on the difficult decision that a young Vietnamese American must make: Should she follow her heart and marry her African American sweetheart, or should she respect her parents' wishes and marry a young immigrant whose cultural background is similar to her own?
	• Before students read the story, pose the following discussion questions:
	  – In a special issue devoted to multiculturalism, *Time* magazine said that the United States is the first nation to develop a genuinely international culture. Do you agree? Why or why not?
	  – If you disagree, do you think that the United States should work to develop an international culture? Explain your reasons.
	• After students read the story, ask them how the characters in "Rain Music" might answer the discussion questions.

All answers are sample answers except those for Vocabulary Practice.

BEFORE YOU READ
Write the Caption

This early Japanese immigrant finds work and success as a farmer.

ACTIVE READING

Taro: Role—shopkeeper, husband, member of Japanese American church; Conflict—whites will not shop at his store; great struggle to succeed

Yamaka: Role—common laborer, member of Japanese American church; Conflict—came from higher society in Japan where he never did the menial work he must do in America

The Todas: common workers, members of Japanese American church; Conflict—must work as a janitor and housecleaner in America; miss the traditions and ways of life of their homeland

Dr. Kaneda: doctor, a leader of Japanese American community; Conflict—despite education and hard work, can never truly achieve American success or status

INTERACTIVE READING
Literary Element: Conflict

Americans resent the Japanese newcomers and regard them as aliens. They will hire the newcomers only as houseboys, cooks, or maids and will not patronize their shops.

Literary Element: Conflict

Hana realizes that American attitudes put her in conflict with her new society. She also experiences internal conflict over her own decision to come to America and to marry. At this point, her internal conflict is more important to her because she regrets her decision to become engaged to Taro, whom she is supposed to marry in only two weeks.

Reading Strategy: Analyze Text Structure

Clues to organization include chapter number, the date, New Year's Day, 1918; all clues to time and the sequence of events, including darkness before dawn and breakfast; and the flashback to the past in Oka Village. These clues tell you that the story will not unfold in strict chronological order. Instead, the order of the story reflects the order of Hana's thoughts.

Reading Strategy: Analyze Text Structure

No, the passage goes back in time to the New Year's feasts of the past that Hana experienced with her family in Japan. The remainder is chronological except for the reference to Hana's earlier insistence to Taro that they have a proper Japanese breakfast on New Year's Day.

ON-PAGE NOTE-TAKING
BIG Idea: Family and Tradition

Students may say that the general acceptance of arranged marriages, as well as Hana's uncle's encouragement of the idea, causes Hana to make the decision. Students may also note that Hana is in some ways rebelling against family and tradition and the way it binds her. They may note how, in her society, male reasoning triumphs over female objections; also, her uncle may want to get rid of her because of her education and spirit.

AFTER YOU READ
Respond and Think Critically

1. Hana agrees to marry Taro because she wants to escape from her village in Japan. She regrets her decision.

2. The Todas are good friends of Taro who take Hana in. Kiku is Americanized and not as traditional as Hana.

3. Their marriage will last because both partners are committed to it and divorce is not a viable option. In time, Hana and Taro may come to truly love each other.

4. Hana does take her role seriously. She demonstrates this when she refuses to continue her relationship with Kiyoshi Yamaka and resolves to be a good wife to Taro.

5. Hana continues to speak her language, enjoy Japanese foods, celebrate in Japanese ways, and recall, with nostalgia, her family and her village.

Apply Background

Students may say that the Introduction helped them realize that "pictures brides" were not unusual among the Japanese in America in the early 1900s.

Literary Element: Conflict

1. She is not in love with or attracted to her husband. She is attracted to another man, Kiyoshi Yamaka.

2. Among the greatest conflicts are the inability to make a living in ways that go beyond menial labor and dealing with the prejudices of Americans, who resent the Japanese Americans' presence and regard them as aliens.

Reading Strategy: Analyze Text Structure

1. The events of the novel begin in 1917 when Hana is on board ship to America. The narrative flashes back to Hana's decision to become a picture bride as well as to a few moments of her childhood in Oka Village.

2. Students may suggest that beginning the story in 1917, when Hana arrives in America, makes sense and that skipping large numbers of years (as reflected by the Table of Contents) will enable the writer to present a greater overview of Hana's life and focus on the most formative events. Students may also reflect historical knowledge of events by noting why an emphasis on 1941–1943 is particularly important in the life story of a Japanese American.

Vocabulary Practice

1. e, 2. c, 3. g, 4. b, 5. f

Academic Vocabulary

Here, *radical* means "relating to extreme change."

Writing

Personal Response

Students' responses should list various challenges and make judgments about how well Hana responds to each of them.

Research and Report

Visual/Media Presentation

Students' visual reports should

- present basic beliefs of Buddhism and Christianity
- explain how each religion was introduced to Japan
- use headings, bullets, and legible type
- include a clear, effective narrative
- use a respectful tone

CHAPTERS 10–23

BEFORE YOU READ

Summarize

Government policies and laws discriminated against not only early Japanese immigrants, Issei, who were not citizens, but also against their children, Nisei, who were citizens.

ACTIVE READING

Mrs. Davis's example: Answers will vary

Author's example: Answers will vary.

Narrator's tone: Students may say *skeptical*

Mary's tone: Students may say *determined, selfish.*

Mrs. Davis's tone: Answers will vary.

Author's tone: Answers will vary.

INTERACTIVE READING

Literary Element: Tone

The tone is one of fear, "ominous overtones" that are first sounded by the visitors' failure to remove their hats in front of a lady. Hana is so distressed at the presence of the men on her porch that she chokes on the English words that would explain Taro's absence.

Literary Element: Tone

The visitors and Taro both express themselves, for the most part, in a matter-of-fact way. The narrator's tone is more sympathetic to Taro, however, who is more polite and accommodating than the men. The visitors initially express a sense of superiority, but they become less and less comfortable in the face of Taro's dignified response. The narrator's tone at the beginning is serious and sympathetic as it evokes Hana's fear at seeing the men. As the passage progresses, the narrator's tone shows increasing respect for Taro's blend of fear and courage.

Reading Strategy: Analyze Historical Context

Whites viewed Japanese Americans as outsiders who could never really integrate into their society. They also actively discriminated against Japanese Americans in public places. They regarded Japanese Americans as people who represented something "other," such as women in kimonos, rather than people who were also Americans.

Reading Strategy: Analyze Historical Context

Mary is ashamed of her mother because society views her as an outsider and an inferior. Miss Nelson views Hana as a nonentity or someone with whom she doesn't have to trouble herself to be polite. Many people of the time and place act in an ignorant and cruel manner toward Asian immigrants.

ON-PAGE NOTE-TAKING

BIG Idea: Family and Tradition

The two families have come to regard each other as real family or "extended family." They are alone, singing traditional songs, stretched out on a traditional mat, and also enjoying the stars, the warm night, and the country. They are all free at this moment from all the cares and woes that a prejudiced society places on them.

AFTER YOU READ
Respond and Think Critically

1. Ellen Davis represents a sympathetic white person. She helps show that not everyone agreed with or practiced discrimination against Japanese Americans.

2. Nishima has had a nervous breakdown, and Hana thinks she can help him. Her actions reveal the caring and generous side of her nature.

3. She is ashamed of her mother's Japanese ways and has little concern for her mother's feelings.

4. Students might say that Hana and Taro are more relaxed and settled in their roles. Their child seems to have brought them closer, and Taro seems appreciative of Hana's work in the shop.

5. They stayed together to be able to speak their own language, to sing their own songs, to express their own values, and to share their own traditions. In some cases, such as that of the Todas and Takedas, they stayed together to replace the families they had left behind with new friends who understood them best.

Apply Background

Students may say that the Background made them realize that racist laws against the Japanese started long before World War II.

Literary Element: Tone

1. Mrs. Davis herself sounds practical and open minded; the narrator describes her with words and phrases such as *regal, warmth,* and *invited friendship*. The tone varies between objective and admiring.

2. While the narrator's tone varies slightly with events, in general it is sympathetic to those characters who either meet with prejudice but hold their heads up and continue to strive, such as Hana and Taro, or who rise above the prevailing prejudice, such as Mrs. Davis.

Reading Strategy: Analyze Historical Context

1. The Takedas can find only certain kinds of jobs; the Takedas can expect people to be rude or prejudiced toward them; the Takedas can expect institutionalized prejudice, such as in their dealings with moving to a house.

2. Students may agree that people act out of ignorance and may cite the "yellow peril" phrase, noting how there was really nothing to fear from characters such as the Todas, Takedas, and others. Students may also conjecture that people's prejudicial actions stemmed from fear or dislike of the "other" in general; after all, prejudice in American history has hardly been limited to Japanese Americans.

Vocabulary Practice

1. dissuade, persuasion

   Dissuade means "to discourage". Persuasion is used to encourage someone to think or act in a certain way.

2. effusive, profuse

   Effusive means "very talkative", or "pouring forth with talk". Something profuse pours forth or is bountiful.

3. erratically, erred

   Erratically means "not consistent", as if in error. *Erred* means "made a mistake or error".

4. impel, propelling

   Impel means "to move forcefully". Propelling means "moving forward".

5. Indignation, dignified

   Indignation means "outrage". Dignified means "composed; not outraged or upset in any way".

Academic Vocabulary

Answers will vary. Students may express excitement at the prospect of a vacation, a concert, or other pleasurable event.

Writing
Write a Letter

Students' letters should be addressed to both Hana and Mary. Letters should explain the differences between them as coming from outside pressures and cultural issues. Letters should suggest ways for Hana and Mary to come together.

Speaking and Listening
Speech

Students' speeches should

• present a list of reasons for putting aside prejudice

• show awareness of the audience and occasion through the use of the pronoun *we* and an informal tone

• be delivered at an effective pace and volume

• be accompanied by one evaluative paragraph about content and a second evaluative paragraph about delivery

CHAPTERS 24–35

BEFORE YOU READ
Write the Caption

The tags worn by these "enemy aliens" reflect the racism and disregard with which they were treated in the process of evacuation and internment.

ACTIVE READING

Tanforan: long lines for meals, showers, laundry, etc.; bad food; lack of privacy; twice-daily head counts; barbed wire; armed guards; FBI searches *Topaz*: located in hot, dusty desert with frequent dust storms; internees live in dusty, drafty barracks; temperatures are cold in mornings, searing hot in afternoons; broken refrigerators, spoiled food; lack of privacy; overcrowded conditions; barbed wire; armed guards Mood at Tanforan: apprehensive, stunned, disbelieving Mood at Topaz: desolation, despair, entrapment

INTERACTIVE READING
Literary Element: Mood

Students may have feelings that range from sympathy for the Todas to a sense of outrage that they should be faced with such a choice. The author uses literary elements such as similes to express the Todas's increasing hopelessness: "Signing with him was like asking a smiling stranger to hold your bag of gold instead of leaving it on the street."

Literary Element: Mood

At first the mood is warm and affectionate as Henry reflects on Kiku. Then the mood begins to change as Henry reflects on his sons' plight. Fear and suspense dominate the mood of the remainder of the passage until Henry is shot, when the reader may experience feelings of shock, horror, or outrage.

Reading Strategy: Visualize

Students may see Hana and Taro sitting on stiff folding chairs, then silently riding the bus through familiar streets, as only the children chatter.

Reading Strategy: Visualize

Descriptive and sensory details include the barbed wire fence, armed guards, the sound of gates swinging shut, the blur of Japanese American faces, the mud and puddles left by the rain, the army barracks everywhere, the stable ramp and numbered doorway, and the whitewashed stall with its two small windows and its smell of horses.

ON-PAGE NOTE-TAKING
BIG Idea: Family and Tradition

Kaneda feels that only in Japan can he be free; only there does he have family, his brother. Taro and Hana, on the other hand, do not think of being repatriated. Their family is in America now, and while they still value their Japanese traditions, they have also accepted America as their home.

AFTER YOU READ
Respond and Think Critically

1. Both Hana and Taro are resigned to the situation and try to make the best of it, although Taro seems more accepting than Hana. Their reactions reveal Taro's stoical nature and Hana's more assertive nature.

2. Taro is shot to death by a guard, who says he thought Taro was trying to escape from camp. Mary is grief-stricken and racked with guilt, reflecting the deep love for her parents that coexists alongside her desire to live an independent life and to fully assimilate into U.S. society.

3. Taro apologizes for not giving Hana a better life; Hana apologizes for the times she has hurt Taro. Students may say the apologies are unnecessary. Taro gave Hana the best life he was able to provide; though Hana hurt Taro when she fell in love with Yamaka, she did her best to make up for it.

4. Some students may say Hana made the right decision because Hana wants to stay near her husband's grave and see to it that he is buried with their son. Others may say that she should leave the camp so she can spend time with her surviving family members.

5. Some students may say that because Kiku and Hana have become like family to each other, and because they are both Japanese American, the ending reflects the Big Idea of family and tradition very well. Others may say that neither woman has a family any more; that all family has been torn from them except each other. Students may also note how their traditions have worked against these women to land them in a kind of prison, made in equal portions of American wartime fears and American prejudice.

Apply Background

Students may say that the fact that the author herself lived in the two "detention centers" described in the novel make her descriptions very believable.

Literary Element: Mood

1. The emotion conveyed by the passage includes anger that the President had made getting rid of the Japanese Americans in California seem like a respectable act.

2. Students may say the mood is hopeful as Hana resolves to carry on and become a citizen, and as she is joyously reunited with Kiku. They "weep for joy," "walk arm in arm," and do not "seem aware of the murky gathering of clouds in the sky" or feel "the ominous gusts of the hot grumbling wind." Students may also say the mood is a mixture of hope and despair, or is ultimately one of despair, by quoting the details above, as well as the final detail about yet another dust storm "enveloping all of Topaz in its white fury."

Reading Strategy: Visualize

1. Students may visualize the dark station at midnight; Mary coming into view in her red coat as she rushes from window to window of the train; Taro and Hana leaning as far out the train car window as they can; the hugging; the brief, excited exchange of words; the gifts of photos, chocolates, and fresh fruit; the hissing steam of the train that forces Joe and Mary to step back; the final reaching out to touch hands; the jerk of the train starting up; the last goodbyes; and Hana's tears.

2. Details include the emphasis on the dust everywhere, including the "mass of dust," the "long dusty road," and being "ankle deep in fine powdery sand." Students may also be able to visualize the "utterly desolate land," "centuries-old bones and stone," and frozen water.

Vocabulary Practice

1. rushed, careless [synonyms]

2. chattered for the entire two-hour ride [explanation/example]

3. for our courage or criticize us for our risk-taking [examples/antonym]

4. damaging the electrical plant was [explanation/general context]

5. those in need by providing food and shelter [explanation/inference]

Academic Vocabulary

A **bond** is a type of interest-bearing security on public or private debt. The first meaning of the word suggests a way in which two people are bound together or united, usually by affection, but also, possibly, simply by shared experience. The second meaning suggests a tie or relationship between an investor, who stands to profit, and a debtor or debtor organization, which needs the help of the investor.

Write With Style

Apply Imagery

Students' descriptions should

• create one main impression of the place

• use spatial order

• include words chosen for their connotations

• use images that appeal to sight as well as to other senses

Speaking and Listening

Debate

Students' debates should

• present clear, well-supported arguments

• anticipate, meet, and undermine counterarguments

• be accompanied by a fairly objective rating

NOVEL AFTER YOU READ

WORK WITH RELATED READINGS

Natsu Okuyama Ozawa—A Japanese Woman Remembers

Like Ozawa, Hana and Taro could not buy a home and were sent to Topaz. Like Ozawa's husband, Taro lost his business. Like Ozawa's son, Hana and Taro's daughter suffered discrimination at school.

from Nisei Daughter

Answers will vary, but students should use excerpts to give a sense of Mary's conflicting feelings regarding her parents and her identity.

Topaz: City of Dust

Hana's reactions to the living quarters, the strong winds and blowing dust of the desert, and the inflexibility of the guards are much like Uchida's.

Sent from the Capital to Her Elder Daughter

Both the speaker and Hana "prize," or value, as well as mourn the loss of, their daughter. Unlike Hana, the speaker seems to face a loss over which her daughter had no control: her daughter was "summoned" by her man. The speaker of the poem also suggests that she is nearly dying from her loss. Hana, on the other hand, is sad but not so desperate: Hana has hopes of being reunited with her daughter at some future time.

Rain Music

Both sets of parents hope that their children will adhere to the conventions of their native culture and will choose spouses who share that culture. These similarities suggest that first-generation Americans may be torn between their allegiance to their parents and native culture and their desire to fit in with mainstream America.

CONNECT TO OTHER LITERATURE

Conflict: The conflict or problem is leaving the place of mists, or forsaking the mists to live somewhere else—in this case, a land without flowers. Hana must decide to forsake her own "mists"—her home and family—to go live in land "without flowers," or one that is unnatural or hostile to her. The mists in the poem may also refer to the mists over Mt. Fuji, a national and cultural symbol of Japan, and the place Hana forsakes.

Tone: The speaker's tone is full of sadness or nostalgia. Mists are forsaken; wild geese fly off; the new place is one without flowers in which geese must "learn" to live, as if living were unnatural there. The narrator's tone in *Picture Bride* is, on the whole, less sad and more objective than the speaker's tone in this poem. The narrator tends to tell the facts of Hana's new life, which are not all bad.

Mood: Students may say that the poem excites feelings of loss. Passages that evoke similar feelings include Hana's reflections on her lost life in Oka Village and her reflections on her daughter once Mary has begun to move away from her emotionally.

Write About it

Hana might write about forsaking her home in Japan and her own family; she might compare the dusty earth in which she now lives as a prisoner to the place without flowers. She might reflect on having learned to deal with, and accept, the harsh conditions of her new life far from the "mists," or far from Japan. She might also compare her youth to a time when she was a wild goose, not content with what she had and eager to fly away.

RESPOND THROUGH WRITING

Research Report

Students' research reports should

- focus on one aspect of East Asian immigration
- be based on reliable, authoritative, timely, and appropriate sources
- present a clear thesis in the introduction
- support, explain, and prove the thesis in the body
- accurately cite and credit sources

All Quiet on the Western Front

Erich Maria Remarque

All Quiet on the Western Front *by Erich Maria Remarque*

All Quiet on the Western Front focuses on a group of German teenagers who enlist to fight in World War I. The novel is a convincing account of the "things seen, heard, and suffered" by the common soldier in the trenches. It poignantly expresses the anger and disillusionment of the generation that survived the horrifying destruction of the war. Because this novel strives to portray the horrors of trench warfare realistically, it includes graphic descriptions of violence and references to bodily functions, which some students may find disturbing.

Synopsis

As the novel begins, a young German soldier named Paul Bäumer and his company have just returned from two weeks of fighting at the front. Only half of the company survived. Among Paul's comrades are several of his former schoolmates, who all joined the army together. The massive bloodshed of the war has quickly rid them of their romantic illusions.

Soon thereafter, the group is trucked to the front line to string barbed wire. Working under constant bombardment, the men rely on instinct to stay alive. Behind the lines, Paul and two comrades, Kropp and Müller, reflect on how the war has ruined their futures. Unlike the older soldiers, the three do not have jobs or families to rejoin. Moreover, their experience of the horrors of the war has made studies and professions seem meaningless.

Soon the men are back at the front to meet an enemy offensive. For days they wait. When the attack begins, the dugouts are blown apart. The men fight like wild beasts.

Attack and counterattack continue for days, but their little piece of earth is held.

Paul is granted leave, but his visit home is a disappointment. His mother is ill with cancer, and Paul feels disconnected from everyone in his hometown. For part of his leave, Paul guards Russian prisoners of war, whom he sees now simply as fellow sufferers.

Returning to his company, Paul is relieved to learn that his closest friends are still alive. The men return to the front, and Paul and several others go on patrol. Alone in a foxhole and pinned down by gunfire, Paul kills a French soldier. He is guilt-ridden as he watches the young man slowly die, but he later justifies the death as a consequence of war.

After an easy assignment in a deserted village, Paul and Kropp are both wounded during an evacuation and are taken to a hospital away from the front. Kropp's leg is amputated, leaving him depressed. Although Paul eventually recovers from his wound, he is overwhelmed by the hundreds of maimed and dying men all around him.

Paul returns to fighting at the front. He clings to the brotherhood among soldiers, but more of his company die. Paul begins to realize that Germany is losing the war. In the summer of 1918, he hears rumors of peace, but the carnage continues. One day, Katczinsky, his last close friend, is wounded. Paul carries him to an aid station, but Katczinsky dies during the journey. Shortly before the armistice, Paul, too, is killed, on a day so quiet that the report from the front says only "All quiet on the Western Front."

Setting the Scene

Help students understand the time and place of the novel's setting.

- Have students do some cursory research on World War I and then create an outline map of Europe during that time period. Have them label all European countries and shade in Germany and Austria. They should also mark the farthest extent of the Western and Eastern Fronts, in France and Russia, respectively. Have them crosshatch the areas of German expansion during the war.

- Because commanders used familiar strategies from earlier periods of warfare, World War I has been called a nineteenth-century war fought with twentieth-century technology. Have students do research and compile an annotated, illustrated list of military technologies employed for the first time during World War I. Students should note how each technology changed warfare.

Visions of War

Prepare students to confront the grim reality of war depicted in the novel.

- Ask students to describe realistic war movies they have seen. What war was the movie about? What scenes in particular conveyed the horror and destruction of the war? Were these scenes of the battlefield or scenes away from the fighting? Ask students if they were moved or shocked by these scenes and why.

- Have students study photographs of World War I scenes showing soldiers, civilians, and medical workers. Have them make generalizations about the war experience based on the photographs. Then have students imagine that they are to be sent from the classroom to an army training camp for ten weeks before being shipped directly into combat. How do they think a person of their age with this amount of preparation would react to the conditions shown in the photographs? If time permits, have students write a journal entry in which they project themselves into a specific photographed scene.

Role-Playing

Introduce students to situations similar to those presented in the novel through role-play.

- Have pairs of students develop a short scene to depict one or more of the following situations:

  - A person has been away from home for a long time. Now his or her feelings toward once-familiar surroundings have changed.

  - A person visits a friend in the hospital. The friend has a serious illness and is feeling depressed about it.

  - Two people have a difficult task to accomplish. They are tired and have not had any food for twenty-four hours.

  - Two people have taken cover during enemy fire and must decide whether to stay in hiding and risk getting caught or run for safety and risk getting shot.

- Give students time to brainstorm the scene they will present. Have several pairs present scenes for each situation.

RELATED READINGS	MAKING CONNECTIONS TO *All Quiet on the Western Front*
Käthe Kollwitz and Vladslo by Jay Winter (Glencoe's *Literature Library*, BLM page 25)	**This selection describes the powerful war memorial created by German artist Käthe Kollwitz for her son who was killed in World War I.** • Before students read, have them give examples of familiar war memorials. Discuss the appearance of each memorial and its effect on viewers. • If possible, show students a photograph of the memorial Käthe Kollwitz created for her son Peter. (See Jay Winter and Blaine Baggett, *The Great War and the Shaping of the Twentieth Century,* a companion book to the PBS film series.) Invite students' comments on the memorial.
Selected Poems by August Stramm, Guillaume Apollinaire, Siegfried Sassoon, and Giuseppe Ungaretti (Glencoe's *Literature Library*, BLM page 26)	**These four poets wrote about their experiences in World War I.** • Before students read, remind them that most of the nations of Europe were involved in World War I. Identify the country associated with each poet. (Stramm—Germany, Apollinaire—France, Sassoon—Great Britain, Ungaretti—Italy) • Suggest that students read each poem aloud at least twice. Have them compare the images of war used by each poet.
The Somme, 1 July 1916: Infantry versus Infantry by John Keegan (Glencoe's *Literature Library*, BLM page 27)	**In this selection, John Keegan gives a historically accurate description of infantry fighting on the Western Front.** • Before students read, introduce John Keegan as a leading military historian who has taken a more humanistic approach to documenting warfare. Traditionally, military history emphasized the study of generals, tactics, and weapons. Keegan instead focuses on what battle was like for the participants and how they coped with danger and the demands that were made on them. • Ask students to take notes on certain points as they read. Tell students to focus on the actions of the soldiers and the overall progress of the battle, rather than on specific names of people or troop units.
Stab in the Back by John Toland (Glencoe's *Literature Library*, BLM page 28)	**This excerpt from Toland's biography of Adolf Hitler reveals a German soldier of World War I who, unlike Paul Bäumer, was enthusiastic and patriotic.** • Suggest that as they read, students watch for the point at which Hitler begins blaming certain groups of people for Germany's woes. Ask them to consider whether the author agrees with Hitler's analysis. • After students read, ask them to explain why they do or do not think that the author shares Hitler's analysis. Then point out that Hitler's rise to power began in 1920, after he joined the German Workers' Party, later renamed the Nazi Party. The party exploited Germans' resentment at losing World War I and the harsh terms of the peace agreement. Widespread dissatisfaction with Germany's chaotic economic situation also helped Hitler's popularity.
Anthem for Doomed Youth by Wilfred Owen (Glencoe's *Literature Library*, BLM page 29)	**This poem emphasizes compassion for the war dead.** • Before students read, point out that Owen's poem is an *elegy*, a poem expressing sorrow or mourning for the dead. • As students read, have them look up any words they do not know. Or you may wish to write selected definitions on the board: *orisons* (prayers), *demented* (insane), *pallor* (ghostly paleness), and *pall* (coffin).

All answers are sample answers except those for Vocabulary Practice.

BEFORE YOU READ

Write the Caption

World War I was a total war that caused hardship, including physical danger, social sacrifices, and food shortages for the people of every involved nation.

ACTIVE READING

Sample answers:

Dialogue: "Mind how you speak to a non-commissioned officer!" bawled Himmelstoss. "Have you lost your senses? You wait till you're spoken to. What will you do anyway?"

"Show you up, Corporal," said Kropp, his thumbs in line with the seams of his trousers.
(Ch. 2)

Effect: reveal personalities

Dialogue: "The Tommies are firing already," says Kropp…

"What's got them?" says Muller, "their clocks must be fast."

"There'll be a bombardment, I tell you. I can feel it in my bones." Kat shrugs his shoulders. (Ch. 4)

Effect: create mood

Dialogue: As I catch hold of the white apron I seize hold of it: "Come quick, Franz Kemmerich is dying."

He frees himself and asks an orderly standing by: "Which will that be?"

He says: "Bed 26, amputated thigh."

He sniffs: "How should I know anything about it, I've amputated five legs today." (Ch. 2)

Effect: create tension

INTERACTIVE READING

Literary Element: Dialogue

Kat expects the new recruits to pay him back for the services he performs. With his closest comrades, however, he does not ask for payback because he feels they already owe each other enough—including their lives.

Literary Element: Dialogue

The fact that the artilleryman laughs at Kropp when Kropp asks about a canteen, or shop, makes Kat even more determined to find food using his special skills. Later he doesn't share the bread with the artilleryman.

Reading Strategy: Evaluate Characters

He takes things as they come and enjoys whatever good he can find in life at the front—whether it's extra food or a momentary light show during artillery fire.

Reading Strategy: Evaluate Characters

Answers will vary. Most students will understand that Detering is simply upset because the horses are innocent and helpless victims caught in the crossfire. Some may note that the soldiers themselves often feel similarly helpless.

ON-PAGE NOTE-TAKING

BIG Idea: Realism and Modernism

Answers will vary. Students might say that there are peculiarly beautiful moments in life even when the circumstances are terrible and that these ordinary moments may be especially pleasurable because of the contrast with the surrounding horrors. Modernist authors sought to convey the gritty realism of everyday life.

AFTER YOU READ

Respond and Think Critically

1. They resent him for having talked them into freely signing up to be soldiers. They now believe they were foolish to listen to him and to follow his advice so blindly.

2. Muller has mixed feelings about the boots. He is sorry for Kemmerich, but he knows Kemmerich is going to die and won't be needing the boots. If Kemmerich dies in the night, the boots will quickly be taken by someone else. But Muller does not want to indicate to Kemmerich that he is not expected to live through the night, so he goes away without the boots.

3. Possible answer: Paul and Katczinsky steal a goose in a slapstick scene and feast together in quiet brotherhood.

4. The men, because of their youth, do not have jobs to return to after the war. Two years of shells and bombs have made them feel that studies and professions are pointless. They don't believe in progress or care about striving for goals anymore.

5. Answers will vary. Students might make reference to loneliness, camaraderie, the death of friends, the intensity of basic training, and the terror and unreality of battle.

Apply Background

Answers may include information about World War I's newly developed weapons of war and the idea of the opposing sides in the conflict holding their ground at all costs, both of which are described in Chapter 4.

Literary Element: Dialogue

1. The men have an easy camaraderie and respect for one another; they are protective of one another in battle.

2. They long for peace, yet they have ceased to believe in the possibility of peace. War has taken its toll on them.

Reading Skill: Evaluate Characters

1. Himmelstoss has very little power over the men at the front. His former trainees are now jaded soldiers, and they no longer fear their former commander. Although Himmelstoss can still have the men arrested or reprimanded, he has essentially lost his power over them.

2. The two men have a way of just being together, without talking, which Paul believes is even more intimate than a love relationship. The simple task of silently roasting a goose in the middle of the night with the war on all sides reveals their deep bond.

Vocabulary Practice

1. The phrases "in front of the advancing troops" and "before the enemy could begin their assault" indicate a military setting and an act of deterrence.

2. The mention of floors, windows, and beds indicates a living place.

3. The context mentions an order and links *refusal* with *insubordination*. The status of the recruits versus the colonel creates a context of authority. This makes it clear that insubordination is disobedience to authority.

4. *Poverty* and an *inheritance of ten thousand dollars* are in direct contrast to one another, which makes it clear that *windfall* means "sudden unexpected gain."

5. *Constant napping* is mentioned as a refutation of *restive*, which indicates that restive means "restless" or at least "wide awake."

Academic Vocabulary

Students may say that hierarchies such as those found in school administrations, boards of directors, and sports teams have benefits, including a clear understanding of position and authority, an organizing principle that allows them to get things done, and so on. Disadvantages might include abuse of power and poor treatment of lower-ranking individuals.

Writing
Write a News Bulletin

Students' news bulletins should be evaluated for

• clarity
• completeness
• use of effective information from the novel.

Research and Report
Visual/Media Presentation

Students' presentations should be evaluated on

• boldness and consistency of graphics
• use of emotional or logical appeals
• organization of information
• public speaking skills

CHAPTERS 6–8

BEFORE YOU READ
Write the Caption

Tanks were introduced during World War I, although they were slow and often got stuck in the mud.

ACTIVE READING

Possible answers: *Sounds:* machine gun barking, the boom of heavy fire, rats shuffling; *Smells:* sulphur fumes, gas, the stench of corpses; *Feelings:* hunger, hot sun, fear; *Sights:* shells flashing, gray light.

INTERACTIVE READING

Literary Element: Description

Students may say they recognize in themselves Paul's sense of sadness, regret, excitement, love of home, and the mixture of pleasure and pain brought about by long-ago memories.

Literary Element: Description

The war has changed Paul; the difference between himself as a boy before the war and now as a man and a soldier makes him feel distant and alienated from those who are not in the same position, even if those people are members of his family.

Reading Strategy: Analyze Style

Similes: *this shadow moves like a ghost* and *the birches stand out again like gay banners on white poles;* sensory language: *stems gleam purest white; airy and silken; pastel green; opalescent blue; shivering breezes; deepens to almost black;* and *red and gold patches of autumn-tinted leaves.*

Reading Strategy: Analyze Style

Students should mention descriptive language. Some may say that the passage is made up primarily of longer sentences. The author's purpose seems to be to reveal Paul's pity, disgust, and sorrow over the peasants' situation.

ON-PAGE NOTE-TAKING

BIG Idea: Realism and Modernism

Paul feels peaceful as long as he does not have to interact with other people, including his father. He knows that his role as a soldier puts him in a special category that only soldiers understand, yet his father and others insist on telling him that things at the front are different from what he knows them to be.

AFTER YOU READ

Respond and Think Critically

1. Paul is surprised because, having seen so much dying, he has become numb to death.

2. Nature's beauty comforts Paul; he intently observes the play of light on the birch trees in a nearby woods. He feels sorry about the hunger and suffering. The Russians do not seem like enemies but fellow victims of their leaders' desire for war.

3. The young women are hungry because of food shortages. Thus, the food the men bring is more important to them than the fact that their visitors are enemy soldiers.

4. Mittelstaedt, now Kantorek's commander, throws Kantorek's patriotic slogans back at him and makes him do menial chores, to Paul's delight. Their treatment of Kantorek, while immature, expresses their anger at squandering their youth in a hellish war.

5. Paul feels anger and bitterness about his mother's illness and the doctors who treat it. He realizes that people who have money settle the price of their treatment in advance, but those who are poor do not dare to ask to—they know they cannot afford it either way.

Apply Background

Students will likely mention the soldiers' ability to recognize the sound of certain kinds of shells during the battle in Chapter 6.

Literary Element: Description

1. The descriptions go from soup kitchens and benches at railway stations to a landscape that is "disturbing, mysterious, and familiar." The names of towns are symbols of his youth. Paul is both excited and bewildered to be back in this place after the traumatic time he has spent at the front.

2. In some ways, Paul seems more comfortable at the front than he does at home with his family. The author's descriptions reveal that being at home makes Paul feel more lonely and alienated from real life than he does at the front as a soldier.

Reading Strategy: Analyze Style

1. Together, the four short sentences create a powerful impression of the men's experience of the calm between storms of artillery fire in an unsafe place. The first-person narration and short sentences add to the immediacy of the situation. The reader feels a part of the scene.

2. Paul's own skin feels like that of a corpse as the cold mist spreads over him and over the dead bodies on the field of battle. The author seems to be making a comparison between the living dead (the soldiers) and the actual dead.

Vocabulary Practice

1. g
2. e
3. b
4. f
5. d

Academic Vocabulary

1. definition: take advantage of; synonyms: use, utilize, make the most of; antonyms: waste, ignore; sentence: The union claimed the company was trying to exploit its workers.

2. The sentence makes clear that the soldiers stop the young recruit from accomplishing his goal. *Restrair* means "to hold back or control."

Write with Style
Apply Description

Students' paragraphs should be evaluated based on their use of interesting words to express a straightforward, unemotional tone. The two paragraphs should contrast with each other—the first should reflect a tone of chaos; the second should reveal a more contemplative take on the same situation or experience.

Research and Report
Internet Connection

Students' reports should

- draw upon multiple research sources
- correlate research with incidents and ideas in the novel
- include completed charts as visual aids
- include accurate and correctly formatted Web site citations

CHAPTERS 9–12
BEFORE YOU READ
Summarize

Soldiers in the trenches of the Western Front endured hardships of all kinds, including constant artillery fire, insufficient food, and illness.

ACTIVE READING

Possible answers:

Return to camp: camaraderie, boredom

Kaiser's visit: disappointment, cynicism

Paul kills soldier: horror, resignation

Paul carries Kat: disbelief, numbness

INTERACTIVE READING
Literary Element: Text Structure

The episode contrasts with Paul's trip home. The sergeant major believes that it is hard to come back to the front after being on leave, but Paul feels that he has become so alienated from civilian life that he is actually more comfortable being back at the army camp than at home with his family.

Literary Element: Text Structure

The effect of the brief episode is one of impending doom, as Paul's horror mounts and he feels confused and terrified. The structure adds to this sense of dread by adding impressionistic horror upon horror.

Reading Strategy: Make Inferences About Theme

Chance or luck is all that stands between life and death.

Reading Strategy: Make Inferences About Theme

This statement reflects the author's antiwar stance. Paul believes that he is no more alive at this point than the soldier he has killed. Killing, he seems to say, is deadly for both the killer and the killed.

ON-PAGE NOTE-TAKING
BIG Idea: Postwar Europe

Remarque's tale is a cautionary one. This is a novel about the terrible numbing effects of war on the human psyche and soul. The title is ironic because Paul's time at the front was anything but quiet except after he died. But in postwar Europe things had quieted down considerably by the time the book was published, and Remarque's title serves a reminder that silence in one moment can be followed by devastation in the next.

AFTER YOU READ
Respond and Think Critically

1. Paul is trapped by enemy fire. He feels guilty. He calls the soldier "comrade," brings him sips of water, and vows not to forget his name. He is trying to relieve his guilt, yet Paul realizes that death is a part of war.

2. One by one nearly all are killed. Germany is losing; the soldiers are starving and the support troops are helpless young boys. The British and American regiments are fresh and large in number and have superior weapons, including tanks.

3. Detering, the farmer, deserts at the sight of cherry blossoms, which remind him of home. Berger enters into No Man's Land to find a wounded messenger dog. Metaphor: "We [soldiers] are little flames poorly sheltered against the storm of dissolution and madness, in which we flicker and sometimes almost go out."

4. Paul has survived ghastly horrors and countless shellings only to die on a quiet day only a month before peace is declared. Students may say the ending made them feel sad, empty, angry, or disillusioned.

5. Paul has lost the will and the desire to live and, like the existentialists, he considers life meaningless. He sees only nothingness in his future; he claims his body moves but the person inside him is long dead.

Apply Background

Students may say that Remarque's wartime experiences lent credibility to the life and times of the soldiers he depicted in the novel.

Literary Element: Text Structure

1. Through small episodes, Remarque reveals Paul's trip home on leave to be even more alienating and lonely than his numbed response to the fighting at the front.

2. Paul kills the soldier in a moment of panic while hiding in the shell-hole; he does not even mean to do it and later claims if he had it to over, he would not have killed him. But things quiet down, as the soldier lies dying. During this quiet time, Paul makes promises to the dead soldier that he knows he will not keep.

Reading Strategy: Make Inferences About Theme

1. To Paul's mind, he and Kat are closer than blood relatives, having shared the pain and hardship of the front for these years. This is related to the theme of comradeship among the soldiers being one of the few positive aspects of war.

2. Students may say one theme is that the stories of all the young soldiers silenced in World War I are left to be told by the war's survivors.

Vocabulary Practice

1. same
2. opposite
3. same
4. opposite
5. opposite

Academic Vocabulary

1. Answers will vary.
2. The phrases "over the course of time" and "inhuman conditions" provide context for the word's meaning, "to get used to."

Writing

Write a Letter

Students' letters should mention incidents from this section of the novel as well as reference thoughts and feelings Paul had while home on leave and his feelings about his future.

Research and Report

Literary Criticism

Students' reports should provide explicit details about the novel and the two pieces of criticism. In addition to subjective opinion, they should back up their ideas with specific examples from the text.

NOVEL AFTER YOU READ

WORK WITH RELATED READINGS

Káthe Kollwitz and Vladso

Through the remarks of the main character, Remarque blames the older generation for the war. Kollwitz's sculpture also expresses the idea that the older generation has betrayed the younger one. Kneeling and bent, her figures suggest the parents' humility and shame; they seem to be begging their son's forgiveness.

Selected Poems

Both "Vigil" and "Battlefield" describe situations or sights similar to those experienced by Paul. However, trapped with the dying French soldier, Paul feels guilt, whereas the speaker in "Vigil" feels a sort of joy sitting next to a dead man. Paul, who describes Kemmerich as childlike and feels outraged by his death, seems to share the perspective and attitude of the speaker in "Battlefield."

The Somme

Remarque's accounts are more compressed. For example, several weeks of fighting are described in a single chapter (6). His accounts present many vivid images of war and emphasize the emotional effects of trench warfare. He does not mention real places. Also, battle is depicted from the point of view of just one soldier. Keegan's account covers one day of battle in detail. He emphasizes the role of human behavior and emotions in the outcome of the fighting, but his account is more technical and factual.

Stab in the Back

He probably would have been relieved by the surrender and dismayed by Hitler's militant patriotism.

Anthem for Doomed Youth

The tone of the poem shifts from bitter anger to tender compassion. The overall tone of the novel is grim, angry, and disappointed. Remarque focuses on the thoughts of living soldiers about their fate; Owen focuses on the dead and calls for a respectful and solemn response to such a great loss.

CONNECT TO OTHER LITERATURE

1. **Dialogue** The dialogue between the soldiers is usually quite spare, while some of the train passengers are verbose. The soldiers speak casually because they have been together a long time. The passengers are strangers to each other, so they speak more formally. Paul's interaction with his father is in some ways similar to the gray-eyed man's discussion of his son's illustrious death—except that the gray-eyed man is covering up his sorrow and Paul's father speaks out of ignorance of the true nature of war.

2. **Theme** Both address the tragedy and the personal loss created by war.

3. **Style** *All Quiet on the Western Front*, except for the final two paragraphs, is written in the first person, from Paul's point of view. "War" has an omniscient third-person narrator.

Write About It

Answers will vary.

RESPOND THROUGH WRITING
Expository Essay

Students' essays should be evaluated on their interesting comparisons and contrasts, their understanding of the two works being compared, and their logical thinking and organization.

Death Comes
for the Archbishop

Willa Cather

Death Comes for the Archbishop *Willa Cather*

Set in nineteenth-century New Mexico, *Death Comes for the Archbishop* tells the story of a French missionary, Bishop Jean Marie Latour. He arrives in Santa Fé in 1851 to discover a vast territory dotted with beautiful red hills and inhabited by Mexicans and Indians who cling to their religious beliefs and customs. Latour struggles to evangelize these people without destroying their own native traditions.

Cather considered the novel among her finest works. Many critics agreed, calling the novel "an American classic." Some, however, argued that the book is not really a novel. Many have criticized it for lacking ambiguity and conflict. Its characters, notes Paul Binding, "move through a wild, undisciplined land and lo! the bad are immediately seen in their badness, the good are rewarded, and the middling feel better for contact with such sanctity." Despite such criticism, *Death Comes for the Archbishop* remains one of Cather's most popular novels.

Before assigning the novel, you may wish to prepare students for the patronizing attitude toward Mexicans and the mistreatment of Native Americans at the hands of early American settlers in the West.

Synopsis

Jean Marie Latour is named Vicar Apostolic of New Mexico. Accompanied by Father Joseph Vaillant, he arrives in Santa Fé only to learn that the Mexican priests there refuse to accept his authority. Latour travels to Durango, Mexico, to acquire proof of his authority. On the way, he suffers from thirst. Miraculously, he discovers a running stream in the Mexican settlement Hidden Water, where he performs marriages and baptizes children.

Father Vaillant is given two beautiful mules on which he and Latour set out for the town of Mora. On the way, they meet an American desperado who plans to rob and kill them. Tipped off by his wife, the two escape to Mora, where the woman exposes her husband as a murderer. He is brought to justice, and Kit Carson takes her in. Latour then visits Padre Gallegos, a degenerate priest, and suspends him. Latour hears the legend of Fray Baltazar, a tyrannical priest who was executed by the Ácoma Indians after he killed an Ácoma servant.

When Father Vaillant becomes seriously ill, Latour goes to his rescue, led by his Indian guide Jacinto. Determined to root out the corrupt priests, Latour expels the Spanish priest Padre Martínez.

Latour's great ambition is to build a cathedral in Santa Fé constructed of golden stone that he discovers on one of his journeys. The dream is to be made possible by a promised bequest from a rich Mexican rancher, Don Antonio Olivares. But when Olivares dies, his surviving brothers contest his will. After helping Don Antonio's widow outsmart them, Latour receives the money to build the cathedral.

Vaillant is sent to Colorado to do mission work in the new mining settlements. When Vaillant dies, Latour recalls his boyhood friend's greatest qualities and reminisces about how the two were joined in pursuing their life's work. Latour asks to be taken to die near the cathedral, which has become a lasting tribute to him.

A Sense of Place

Help students connect *Death Comes for the Archbishop* with their own life experiences.

- Tell students that Willa Cather is renowned for conveying a strong sense of place in her writing.

- Share a passage from Cather's novel as evidence. Have students identify the techniques that Cather uses to paint word pictures of the American Southwest, as well as of southern Italy and France.

- Have students think about a place to which they feel deeply connected. Ask them to describe what images, thoughts, and feelings come to mind as they think about the place.

- Ask students to describe in writing a place that they love. Encourage them to enrich their description with imagery and figurative language.

Exploration and Annexation

Provide a brief overview of New Mexico's history.

- Explain that *Death Comes for the Archbishop* is set after the Mexican-American War (1846–1848) and the ceding of New Mexico to the United States. Point out that New Mexico was part of Mexico from 1821 to 1848 and before that was occupied by Spain.

- Explain that the Spaniard Fray Marcos de Niza first explored New Mexico in 1539 and was followed by his countryman Francisco Vásquez de Coronado in 1540. Don Juan de Oñate established the first permanent Spanish settlement in 1598.

The Seven Sacraments

Familiarize students with the sacraments of the Catholic Church.

- Explain that the Catholic Church recognizes seven sacraments, or Christian rites considered to be outward signs of inner spiritual grace. Provide a short definition of these sacraments: baptism, confirmation, Eucharist, reconciliation, holy orders, marriage, and anointing of the sick.

- Ask each student to choose one sacrament to research and then to write a paragraph describing the function that it serves in a Catholic's faith life.

American Archaeology

Have students read archaeological studies from the late 1800s and early 1900s.

- Point out that Cather read studies by anthropologists and archaeologists on New Mexico's Indian tribes. Have students select one of the following studies to read:

  – Charles Lummis's *Mesa, Cañon, and Pueblo* (1925).

  – Edward S. Curtis's *The North American Indian* (1907–1930).

  – Haniel Long's *Notes for a New Mythology* (1926).

- After students have finished reading, have them present brief oral reports on their findings. Then have them tell how their reading enhanced their understanding of Cather's novel.

RELATED READINGS	MAKING CONNECTIONS TO *Death Comes for the Archbishop*
On *Death Comes for the Archbishop* by Willa Cather (Glencoe's *Literature Library*, BLM page 24)	**Cather wrote this letter to answer readers' questions about the historical sources she used in writing *Death Comes for the Archbishop*.** • You may wish to use this as a postreading activity for *Death Comes for the Archbishop*. • After students have read the letter, have them discuss whether or not they believe Cather achieved the goals that she set for herself in writing the novel. Have them cite evidence from the novel that shows she achieved what she set out to do.
Through Tewa Eyes: Origins by Alfonso Ortiz (Glencoe's *Literature Library*, BLM page 25)	**This article by a Tewa Pueblo Indian provides insight into Tewa customs and beliefs.** • You may wish to use this article as a prereading activity for Book Four, Chapter 2, of the novel, in which Latour and Jacinto spend the night in a kiva. • Encourage students to apply what they learned from the article on Tewa culture to help them understand the role that the kiva plays in the novel and the respect that Jacinto has for it.
In 1864 by Luci Tapahonso (Glencoe's *Literature Library*, BLM page 26)	**The relocation of the Navajo that took place in 1864 is an event described in both this poem and Cather's novel.** • You may wish to use this poem as a prereading activity for Book Nine, Chapter 7, of the novel, in which the Navajo's expulsion from their own country is described. • After students have read Chapter 7, invite them to share their opinions as to whether or not the poem's depiction of the Navajo's evacuation is more moving than Cather's description. Have them support their opinions with details from both works.
Holy Sonnet 167 by John Donne (Glencoe's *Literature Library*, BLM page 27)	**Like the character Latour, this poem's speaker faces death unafraid.** • You may wish to use this poem as a postreading activity for *Death Comes for the Archbishop*. • Ask students to describe the speaker's attitude toward death. Which words best express the tone. or attitude? • After students have read the poem, ask them if their attitude toward death has been influenced by the speaker's argument. Why or why not?
American Odyssey: Cycling the Santa Fe Trail by Dennis L. Coello (Glencoe's *Literature Library*, BLM page 28)	**This article describes a man's bicycle tour along the Santa Fe Trail.** • You may wish to use this as a prereading activity for *Death Comes for the Archbishop*. The Santa Fe Trail plays a significant role in the novel. • Before students read the article, ask them to identify facts about the trail, where it begins, and where it ends. List responses on the board. • After students have read the article, have them tell what they learned about the Santa Fe Trail.

All answers are sample answers except those for Vocabulary Practice.

PROLOGUE, BOOKS 1–2

BEFORE YOU READ
Summarize

Cather populates her novel with a historically accurate mix of cultures and with some actual historical figures, including Kit Carson.

ACTIVE READING

Sabine Hills: hidden garden; declivity planted with vineyards; potted orange and oleander trees; shaded by spreading ilex oaks; landscape stretched soft and undulating; supreme splendour; shining folds of country; bright green of orange trees; the rose of oleander blooms; waves of rose and gold throbbed up the sky. Mood: splendor.

Central New Mexico: monotonous red sand-hills; so many uniform hills; country no more changed than if he had stood still; thirty miles of conical red hills; began to think he would never see anything else; they were so exactly like one another, he seemed to be wandering in a geometrical nightmare; uniform yellowish green, as the hills were a uniform red; blunted pyramid, repeated so many hundred times. Mood: monotony.

Truchas Mountains: an icy wind; slate-coloured mountain meadows; horny backbones of mountains; purplish lead-coloured clouds; dark vapours; cold green of the evergreens; faces of the two priests were purplish and spotted; grey daylight. Mood: foreboding.

INTERACTIVE READING
Literary Element: Setting

The cruciform tree, or tree in the shape of a cross, is symbolic. The traveler kneels before it to pray. Students may also interpret other aspects of the setting as symbolic, such as the sameness or uniformity and the color red.

Literary Element: Setting

The Fathers' journey has been a great ordeal. As the Fathers approach Santa Fé, the sun is setting and bathing the Villa, Santa Fé, in red, the color of the blood of Christ. The town and its church rise out of a depression in the land, bathed in red light, and also dotted with the greenery of life. Santa Fé rises up, sanctified, as a symbol of life or holiness.

Reading Strategy: Draw Conclusions About Culture

Students may note that the Europeans in this passage think they know more about the local people than the local people do. They may suggest that the Europeans feel superior and certain of their right to decide what is best for others.

Reading Strategy: Draw Conclusions About Culture

Students should note the many prejudices exposed in this passage about French, German, and Spanish people. The fact that the cardinals are trapped in their own stereotypes about cultures they know suggests that they will not deal fairly with cultures of which they are ignorant.

ON-PAGE NOTE-TAKING
BIG Question: Cultures in Conflict

Problems include the "haughty and suspicious" Indians, a cultural conflict arising from misunderstanding, possibly on both sides; the refusal of the Mexican congregation to have its children baptized, a cultural conflict arising from past treatment by the Spaniards; the material problem of the bad horse, which may point to a culture in which deceit is frequently practiced upon the unwary; the rancho system, as evidenced by Lujon and his place, where children may have no other clothing but their shirts and where the rich man decides and controls all, including when or if people will be married.

AFTER YOU READ
Respond and Think Critically

1. The Mexican priests in Santa Fé refuse to accept his authority. Latour decides to set off for Durango to acquire the necessary papers. He is revealed to be a composed, intelligent, and determined man.

2. Latour, suffering from thirst, discovers a running stream and human fellowship in Agua Secreta. He perceives the people as ignorant but faith-filled.

3. Latour gives Magdalena decent clothes, protects her from Scales, and finds a home for her. Magdalena represents Mary Magdalene, as she is "redeemed" by a man of God.

4. The two mules symbolize the close relationship between Vaillant and Latour. The two mules are inseparable, just as Vaillant and Latour are.

5. Many answers are possible. There is tension between the French missionaries and the local Mexican people in part because of the past problems with Spanish priests. There is tension between the Spanish landowner, who was

accustomed to dealing with Spanish clerics, and the new French clerics.

Apply Background

Students may note that Cather had actually experienced the land and people of the place she writes about. They may also note that the information about Catholic officials, dioceses, and missions helped them sort out people, roles, and chains of command in this first section of the novel.

Literary Element: Setting

1. Details of the setting such as "dry ashes," "dead-looking cactus," "sand curling about them," and "a cold wind" all create a sense of a hostile landscape that may overpower the men before they achieve their goals.

2. Many answers are possible. Critics have pointed to the brilliant red of the sky at sunset as symbolic of the blood of Christ, by which they mean the passion, or Christ's suffering on the cross. Students may associate the sunset with the end of one day, or era, and the promise of a new beginning, as in the kind of spiritual new beginning that the cardinals and the missionaries hope to effect.

Reading Strategy: Draw Conclusions About Culture

1. Students may argue that a belief in miracles unites the characters. They may cite the "miracle" of water at Agua Secreta, the miracle of the Blessed Virgin that Padre Herrera describes, and the miracle in the story of Mary Magdalene.

2. Students will likely say they are quite well suited. Father Latour shows perseverance when the prevailing Catholic culture refuses to recognize his authority. He looks kindly upon the people he meets in Agua Secreta. Both priests make every effort to speak with the native people in their own language. Both priests do not expect or strive for comforts and undertake long missionary journeys that are difficult. Father Vaillant knows how to get what he needs from the rich in his new land, as in the story of the two mules.

Vocabulary Practice

1. robbing a store
2. when the person has greatly displeased you
3. someone who takes great risks
4. snacking every night in front of the television
5. while standing at the top of a cliff

Academic Vocabulary

its religious head, the pope; cardinals, who may be bishops in their own dioceses or advisers to the pope at the Vatican in Rome; and priests, who lead local parishes.

Writing
Write with Style

Students' essays should

- describe a setting
- create a single dominant emotional impression of a place
- use at least one symbol that conveys the dominant emotional impression
- organize ideas in a spatial order that is appropriate to the topic

Connect to Content Areas
Art

Students' reports should

- focus on at least one Spanish, one Mexican, and one Native American artist who created works that may have found their way to the New Mexico Territory by 1851
- describe each artist's style and influences
- use appropriate subheadings
- include a Works Cited list, in-text citations, and source lines for any visuals
- explain any technical or unfamiliar terms
- be presented with appropriate and effective verbal and nonverbal techniques

BOOKS 3–6
BEFORE YOU READ
Write the Caption

Pueblos of the Southwest were actually small villages made up of several buildings that stood up to three stories high.

ACTIVE READING

Padre Gallegos—Sin: sloth; Details: won't attend Bishop on trip to the missions; won't celebrate mass at Ácoma; Others' Responses: suspended of all priestly functions; Evaluation: Effectively shows priest who has lost touch with his basic responsibilities

Friar Baltazar Montoya—Sins: gluttony, pride; Details: takes the best of Indians' corn, beans, squash, sheep parts, and hides; drains their water supply for his garden; sends Indian servants to bring him the best of everything; drinks too much grape brandy and kills Indian servant; Responses: Indians throw him over mesa; Evaluation: Vividly and dramatically shows punishment for sin

Padre Martínez—Sin: lust; Details: doesn't practice celibacy; ruins a Mexican girl; Responses: is asked to resign his parish; forms own church after clashing with new priest; is formally excommunicated; Evaluation: Effectively shows sin and corruption

Father Lucero—Sin: avarice; Details: wrings pesos out of Mexican parishioners; kills young man who tries to rob him; keeps money he is given to say masses for the repose of Martínez's soul; Responses: forms new church with Martínez; is excommunicated; is reconciled to the Church before dying; Evaluation: Clearly shows how priests have been left on their own to make and follow their own rules

INTERACTIVE READING
Literary Element: Voice

The narrator is observant and nonjudgmental about the home, appreciative of the cleanliness and sweet-smelling smoke. The word choices convey sympathy for the tribe that is dying out and to Jacinto's sick baby, less sympathy for the "dark legends." Students may describe the voice here as tender yet reserved; interested and human yet distanced.

Literary Element: Voice

Descriptive language that stresses abundance, including "streams were full of fish, the mountain was full of game," helps create contrast with word choices such as *empty* and *ruined* and emphasize the sense of loss. The cataloguing of deadly diseases and the legend of young babies sacrificed to a snake convey a feeling of horror at the fate of the once numerous tribe. The meditative mood at the end of the passage, accompanied by the "feeble wailing of the sick child in the cradle," convey a sense that the author feels measured sympathy for the plight of these people.

Reading Strategy: Evaluate Characterization

Cather chooses direct characterization because the words and thoughts of these characters are of no importance in this scene. The banjo player is a kind of stock character or stereotype; the word *yellow* is meant to classify him as a Mexican, and the details reduce him to a kind of mechanical prop in this scene. Kit Carson functions as an archetypal character, the larger-than-life trail-breaker and scout with "far-seeing

eyes." Cather tells all the reader needs to know with these few details.

Reading Strategy: Evaluate Characterization

Chavez is the "disdainful" Spaniard, descended from past glory, and rich in land and authority in the "New World." He is at odds with the Americans, from whom he is as different as night is from day, as evidenced by such details as his elegant dress and his use of a bow and arrow. The details about hunting Navajos for sport, as well as for vengeance, economically show his great disdain for, distrust of, and hatred of the native people.

ON-PAGE NOTE-TAKING
BIG Idea: Cultures in Conflict

Father Ramirez appears to have viewed the native people as servants or slaves in service of his own glory. He has forced men, women, and children to carry the materials for his church a distance of forty or fifty miles. Latour views the native people as a "tribe of ancient rock-turtles." They are not "his own kind" and they do not the share the "glorious" European history of "desire and dreams." Instead, to him, they are "rock-turtles on their rock."

AFTER YOU READ
Respond and Think Critically

1. The bishop doesn't want to be impolite and doesn't believe that he could understand Jacinto's culture or that Jacinto could understand his.

2. Friar Baltazar is tyrannical, overbearing, hot-tempered, ambitious, and greedy. When the friar's Indian serving boy spills gravy on a visiting priest, the friar throws a mug at the boy, killing him. The Acomas avenge the boy's death by executing the friar. Despite Baltazar's actions, the Indians respect him.

3. Madame Olivares is vain. Father Vaillant urges her to forget her vanity, warning her that she could be left poor. Latour flatters her, saying that she is only as old as she looks. Vaillant is impulsive, straightforward, sharp-tongued, and impatient; Latour is gentle, patient, and smooth.

4. Students may say that the author's use of legend in the narrative adds believability and authenticity to the Native Americans who are portrayed in the story.

5. The white men think the Pecos are dying out because their young men's strength is being sapped by keeping a sacred flame and because Pecos babies are being sacrificed to a great snake. The real reason that they are dying is that smallpox and measles are afflicting them. Latour is uncomfortable with the pagan traditions of the Pecos people.

Apply Background

Students may say that the information in Build Background helped them understand the pueblos and peoples of Ácoma and Pecos.

Literary Element: Voice

1. The voice of the narrator is heard primarily through description, especially of the landscape, but also of homes and other places, as well as through narration. Although there is some dialogue, it does not evoke the narrator's personality as much as description and narration do.

2. The narrator admires both priests. The narration reveals their almost always laudable emotional responses to events. For example, Father Vaillant is "scandalized" by Father Lucero's lax morals, and Father Latour feels "a little ashamed" about all the work the sisters in Clermont must do to sew their vestments. Father Latour uses few words, but when he speaks to Father Martinez, he does so with clarity, firmness, and authority.

Reading Strategy: Evaluate Characterization

1. The words, thoughts, and actions of Father Latour are most frequently heard; Vaillant is also frequently characterized through his words, thoughts, and actions. Lesser characters are revealed more through indirect rather than direct characterization.

2. The novel does use conventional characterization, although it relies far less on dialogue, or the characters' own words, as a method of characterization than many novels do.

Vocabulary Practice

1. same
2. same
3. opposite
4. opposite
5. opposite

Academic Vocabulary

1. definition: to bring into view, to make visible
2. synonyms: expose, bare, show, display, uncover
3. antonyms: conceal, hide, cover
4. sentence: The robber refused to reveal the hiding place.

Writing

Summarize a Legend or Myth

Students' summaries should

• begin with the title and source of the myth

• include the main characters, setting, problem or conflict, main events, and resolution but omit unimportant details

• be no longer than one third the length of the original story

• conclude with a statement contrasting voice

Connect to Content Areas

Math

Students' reports should

• include a chart or spreadsheet that shows and totals the distances traveled

• explain how the distances you calculated, as well as those reported in the novel, may vary from actual distances traveled and why

BOOKS 7–9

BEFORE YOU READ

Write the Caption

The members of this Navajo family probably refer to themselves as the Dine.

ACTIVE READING

1. May 1859– Father Vaillant is recovering from illness in Santa Fé (present).

2. December 1859– Bishop Latour experiences doubts (present), Latour recalls times in the past related to his cloak (flashback), Sada escapes her employers to visit Father Vaillant (episode), Incidents of the past related to Sada (past)

3. Spring 1860– Latour visits Eusabio (present), Latour recalls his seminary days, including various moments with Vaillant and Vaillant's visit to the Pope (flashbacks)

4. 1860– Eusabio and Latour ride back to Santa Fe together (present), Latour reflects on Native American ways (present)

INTERACTIVE READING

Literary Element: Plot

1. These paragraphs help convey rising action by pointing to a problem and its possible solution. Students may, however, note that this rising action creates little narrative tension and that the incorporation of historical elements seems just as important here as any possible movement of the plot.

2. A flashback occurs as Father Vaillant slips into a memory of a man condemned to death for murder and his final action of making a pair of tiny boots for Santiago of Chimayo. The scene shows Father

Vaillant's sympathy for the murderer, a young man who acted out of passion, not premeditation.

Reading Strategy: Recognize Bias

1. Father Latour has great admiration for the Indians and lauds their respect for the land, caution, and discretion. His bias is mainly positive, but there are tinges also of negativity. For example, students may say that that statement that "Indians disliked novelty and change" is not only an oversimplification but also, given European sensibilities of right and wrong, a criticism. Similarly, the comment about their "exhaustless patience" in working silver contains within it judgments about how much time and effort should be expended on the working of silver. Even when Latour thinks that the Native American accommodation to the landscape is not a matter of laziness, he qualifies the statement and adds a trace of negativity by saying that their accommodation was "*not so much* [emphasis added] from indolence."

2. The thoughts of Father Vaillant express a bias in favor of the Mexicans and their generosity. The passage shows how Mexican women, in particular, are sympathetic to Vaillant and his needs, especially when they involve living with "improprieties."

ON-PAGE NOTE-TAKING
BIG Idea: Cultures in Conflict

This passage details the fate of the Navajos, which resulted from the westward expansion of the United States: they were hunted down and driven from their own lands by whites, and specifically by Kit Carson, who subdued almost all of them except Manuelito and a few followers.

AFTER YOU READ
Respond and Think Critically

1. Vaillant doesn't show regret over leaving his friend, whereas the separation pains Latour deeply. Vaillant makes friends easily while Latour does not.

2. Latour tends his garden and trains new missionaries who arrive from France. The light, dry wind in New Mexico makes him feel young, whereas France makes him feel old.

3. Latour remembers the time that he and Vaillant left Clermont, Vaillant's funeral, his winters in France, his student days, and the building of the cathedral. These scenes had great emotional effects on his life.

4. The statement is an oversimplification. Anyone who has compassion can understand the suffering of others, regardless of gender.

5. Cather is sympathetic toward Native American rights. She shows the bishop to be a highly moral man and she shows the bishop's great sympathies for Jacinto, Eusabio, and other Native Americans throughout the novel. She shows the bishop meeting with Manuelito even though it is against the law and says he does it because he is "a man, too, and a lover of justice."

Apply Background

The background information helps explain the Navajo's territory, their fighting spirit, the loss of their lands, and the fighting that involved Carson and Manuelito.

Literary Element: Plot

1. Students may cite these episodes and others: the story of the servant woman and devout Catholic Sada; legends of snakes that take babies; meetings with various corrupt priests and two murderers.

2. The term *modernism* applies because of the novel's unconventional structure. Although the general pattern of the story is chronological, the plot does not lead up, event by event, to a single climax, nor does it create and then dispel narrative tension. Instead, many stories and episodes are merged, and some character development is achieved by means of flashbacks.

Reading Strategy: Recognize Bias

1. Students may say that Father Vaillant's work in Colorado (then part of the Utah Territory) provides necessary help to the men who flocked there. They may note various ways in which the Fathers gave solace and hope to the poor or outcast, such as Sada and Magdalene. They may say that the Church, with its many churches and cathedrals, as much as the government and entrepreneurs, helped build the Southwest as we recognize it today. Students may also say that the church helped unify disparate cultures by bringing them into the same family of belief or worship.

2. Father Latour believes in the church and his faith as right for everyone and as a force for good. He transcends the biases of his time by seeing qualities to respect in the Native Americans and feeling outraged at the injustice they suffered, but he also maintains some bias about their otherness or about them as a kind of separate race.

Vocabulary Practice

1. B, 2. B, 3. A, 4. A, 5. B

Academic Vocabulary

In the sentence, *convert* means to change the units of a quantity. Both meanings suggest a type of change, but one is specific to religion or belief systems, and the other to an expression of quantity in alternative units.

Writing

Write a Treatment

Students' treatments should

- present a plot outline for a movie or TV version of the novel
- include a cast of characters with their most important traits and suggestions for actors who might portray them
- suggest settings or a style of filming to create the appropriate atmosphere
- be addressed to studio executives

Research and Report

Literary Criticism

Students' reports should

- present a clear thesis statement that responds fully to the passage of literary criticism
- include logical, persuasive arguments
- be presented using appropriate verbal and nonverbal techniques
- be accompanied by a paragraph of self-evaluation

AFTER YOU READ

WORK WITH RELATED READINGS

On *Death Comes for the Archbishop*

Like Lamy, Latour is well bred, distinguished, energetic, and optimistic in the face of hardship.

Through Tewa Eyes: Origins

The customs of living in house blocks, building religious sanctums in the mountains, and keeping certain information within the tribal community all are mentioned.

In 1864

Tapahonso presents Carson as an evil, heartless man, whereas Cather presents him as a tender, intelligent man.

Holy Sonnet 167

Both writers present death as a peaceful event not to be feared but rather to be embraced.

American Odyssey: Cycling the Santa Fe Trail

In the 1850s, travelers were likely to be attacked by Indians.

CONNECT TO OTHER LITERATURE

Setting: In "A Walk to the Jetty," the setting is the location of present events, and aspects of the setting also act as triggers for the narrator's recollections. In *Death Comes for the Archbishop,* the setting is also sometimes a trigger for flashbacks for both Latour and Vaillant; more commonly, it is the location of the present action and, at times, symbolic of Latour's challenges, faith, and life's work.

Voice: With its first-person narration, the voice in "A Walk to the Jetty" is very intimate, revelatory, and personal. The voice in *Death Comes for the Archbishop* is more formal and removed; nevertheless, there is some tenderness or softness toward the characters.

Plot: Both works have a nontraditional plot. "A Walk to the Jetty" reveals character and conflict through flashbacks. *Death Comes for the Archbishop* reveals character and tells a life story, as well as a brief history of the Southwest, through a series of stories or episodes and some flashbacks.

Talk About It

Students may say that both works involve a physical journey (there is just one physical journey in "A Walk to the Jetty"; there are many physical journeys in the novel). Students may also say that the journeys have a mental or emotional quality to them. In "A Walk to the Jetty," the walk, or journey, is a time for reflecting in great detail on the narrator's past. In the novel, most of the journeys are undertaken for the priests' professional and therefore spiritual purposes, but some of them become opportunities for personal reflection or growth. Students who have read all of "A Walk to the Jetty" may add other comparisons and contrasts.

RESPOND THROUGH WRITING

Short Story

Students' short stories should

- include a setting that is integral to the events or has symbolic aspects
- create distinctive atmosphere
- present a conflict or problem and a series of connected events that rise to a climax